JAMES LUMSDEN & SON
OF GLASGOW

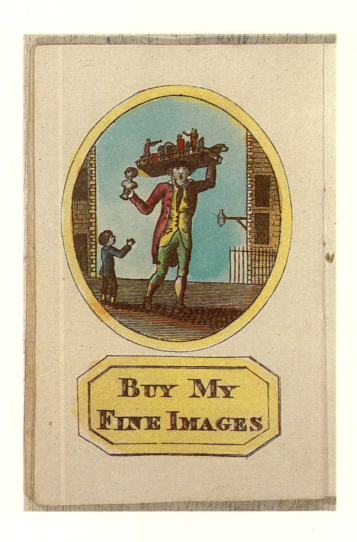

# JAMES
# LUMSDEN
## & SON OF GLASGOW

Their Juvenile Books and Chapbooks

# S. ROSCOE
# &
# R. A. BRIMMELL

PRIVATE LIBRARIES ASSOCIATION

1981

S. Roscoe & R. A. Brimmell © 1981
Published by the Private Libraries Association
Ravelston, South View Road, Pinner
Middlesex, England

Distributed in the U.S.A. and Canada by
Justin G. Schiller, Ltd.
36 East 61st Street, New York, N.Y. 10021

Printed and bound in Great Britain by
Clark Constable Ltd, Edinburgh
Designed by David Chambers

2,000 copies, of which 750 are for sale
SBN 900002 04 2

*Reversible head on half-title*
*from Item No. 20, Tommy Thumb's Song Book, 1815.*
*(Courtesy Peter Stockham at Images.)*
*Frontispiece from No. 105, The New Cries of London.*
*(Courtesy The Museum of Childhood, Edinburgh.)*

# CONTENTS

# PREFACE

The late Sydney Roscoe commenced making notes for a bibliography of the juvenile publications of James Lumsden & Son of Glasgow in the early 1950s. It was a secondary interest to the main one of his major work *John Newbery and his Successors*. By the time this was completed he had been struck down with illness and was living in a Nursing Home in St. Leonards on Sea. We often discussed our mutual enthusiasm for Lumsden, and when it became obvious he could never finish the work, which caused him considerable distress, I offered to take over his notes and complete the book.

I wish to make it quite clear that although I have written up the notes, added a good deal in the way of information about the publications and located a number of new titles this is his book. He conceived it and did all the ground work. I have merely tried to follow in his footsteps and complete the book as he would have wished, and I like to think that he gained a measure of comfort in those last months from the knowledge that his work would not go for nothing and that the book would be completed and published.

Generally we were in complete agreement on conclusions to be drawn from the scanty information available. Only on one point do we cross swords — S.R. was firmly of the opinion that James Lumsden, junior, was only interested in the social activities related to his public life, and did not play a very active part in the running of the business of James Lumsden and Son. I am far from convinced of this fact for as is pointed out in the Introduction he was in the firm during its most productive period and did not apparently enter public life until long after the death of James, senior. S.R. based his opinion mainly on the strength of the rather clumsily written letter to Thomas Bewick (see Introduction) which suggested to him that the writer was not the sort of person to have produced the charming Lumsden juveniles. However, the points he makes in the letter are perfectly practical and it must be remembered that styles have changed in business communication. Therefore in the Introduction I have left conclusions as to his participation in the publishing side of the business open for want of firmer evidence.

On other matters I am quite satisfied that his conclusions are correct. I have examined the illustrations in a large number of Lumsden publications, and feel sure his view that they contain no cuts by Bewick is generally accurate. Two entries in Bewick's

*Weekly Engraving Book* 1791-7 [Laing Gallery R34] for May 14 and June 4, 1791 record cuts for Whittington and Robinson Crusoe. Whether they were ever used or not is open to conjecture as no copies of these titles earlier than about 1815 have been located or even traced from advertisements. In my opinion all the cuts examined in surviving copies of their publications are the work of local Glasgow cutters in his employment who may have consciously attempted to imitate the master. There has always been some doubt as to the accuracy of a number of Hugo's attributions, and I fear that collectors who have bought Lumsdens on the assumption they contained Bewick cuts must now accept the fact that they have been misled and lick their wounds. S.R. did suggest the *Juvenile Drawing Books* series might be the work of Bewick, but he had only examined photostats. I have now acquired some half-dozen titles in the series and although I must acknowledge at once that they are far and away the best illustrated of all Lumsden books — the work is that of an excellent professional artist — I can see no grounds for assuming they are by Bewick for the style appears to be rather different, and, moreover, Bewick is not known to have used the soft ground process.

It must be emphasised that the present volume makes no claim to be a complete list of Lumsden Juvenile publications. Apart from a few titles they are extremely scarce. Many have vanished completely from the market and have only been listed from advertisements, but one hopes that time and the rising interest in their publications will result in other titles coming to light. As far as possible descriptions have been kept to a uniform style favoured by S.R. but it will be appreciated that in many cases we have had to rely on information kindly passed on by librarians and collectors who are at some distance — often abroad — who have given their time to providing details of copies in their possession but could not be expected to work to a standard format. In these cases obviously there may be slight variations of style in description.

R. A. Brimmell, Hastings, 1978.

# ACKNOWLEDGEMENTS

The late Mr Roscoe was particularly indebted to Mr Leslie Shepard for informing him of sources of information about the Lumsdens, father and son, for which he had long searched in vain. Best thanks go to him, to Mrs Marjorie McNaughtan who has helped with research in Edinburgh, and to all those librarians, curators, collectors and dealers who have helped us to find copies, and to those named below who have kindly allowed reproductions to be made from their copies, where not available in our own collections.

Aberdeen University Library

British Library (British Museum)

Bodleian Library

Cambridge University Library (by permission of the Syndics)

Glasgow University Library

John Johnson collection (now in the Bodleian Library)

Museum of Childhood, Edinburgh

National Library of Scotland (by permission of the Trustees)

The Osborne Collection, Toronto Public Library

St. Andrews University Library

Sheffield University Library

Victoria and Albert Museum, London

# INTRODUCTION

Little information regarding the firm of James Lumsden and Son has survived. No records of the firm are to be found, and it has even proved impossible to give dates to the birth and death of the founder of the firm, James Lumsden, senior. Indications are that he was probably born about 1750-5 and died about 1830. In his early years he was described as an engraver, and a lucrative part of his business was the publication of cheap hand-coloured pictures of Sir William Wallace, Rolla, Young Norval, Flora MacDonald and other popular characters. He published a plan of the City of Glasgow in 1783, and it would seem his earlier publishing activities were confined to commercial printing of all kinds, steamboat tickets, tide tables, bills etc. The firm were undoubtedly general stationers in a large way of business.

It would seem they first became interested in publishing books for children about the end of the eighteenth century, but their scarcity is probably accounted for by the fact that distribution was purely local — there is no hint that any serious attempt was made to invade the English market which was already well provided for by Newbery, Harris, Marshall and others. In their own way the Lumsden books show a distinctive quality; it is not easy to define and does not hold in all cases, though, with exceptions a Lumsden is easily recognisable to the experienced eye. It is a certain trimness (primness one might almost call it) in the covers, the quality of the paper used, the excellent type-face, the occasional use of coloured inks for text and illustrations, usually bistre or sanguine, occasionally green, and a few hand-coloured illustrations. This use of coloured inks produced some very charming results, viz: *Fun upon Fun* (No. 72). Another attraction was the paper covers or wrappers used. In the specifications of books it will be noted that books were issued in a variety of coloured wrappers — not one colour for each book, but perhaps half a dozen; a most attractive trick not met with elsewhere except in the miniature boxed books for children, *The Infant's Library* and others of that species. *Fun upon Fun* can be found in jackets of green, brown, pink, grey-green, orange-pink, drab, blue-grey, all at the same price.

There are carefully engraved labels on the upper covers, or well-designed woodcuts, often on both covers. The woodcuts on the lower covers sometimes take the form of rather unlovely reversible heads, great fun to design and very amusing for many

xi

children, but repulsive and frightening for others. These woodcuts are not always appropriate to the text, a fault common enough in children's books. The reversible heads on Watts' *Divine Songs*, 1814 (No. 38) represent 'laughter' and in the reverse, 'anger', which rather lets down the Lumsden standard. Sometimes a lower cover repeats the title and has a general advertisement of Lumsden productions.

Other publishers produced books of equal charm; the Newberys, with their brightly coloured Dutch floral paper wrappers, tinted with a thin overwash of gold (very seldom seen now, as handling was fatal to its existence) and then woodcuts and engravings; the dainty pages of John Marshall's *Poems on Various Subjects for the Amusement of Youth* (in or before 1783), each poem headed by an oval woodcut, of graceful design, framed at top and sides with ropes of foliage, or his *Cobwebs to Catch Flies*, of similar date and design in two volumes, with its lively cuts of the children at the fair. Then, a little later came the fashion for boxes of books, *The Infant's Library*, already mentioned of about 1800 and later, sixteen tiny books for little children, also by Marshall, Wallis's *Bookcase of Instruction* in ten very small volumes (1813), and others. Some firms gave away a box to purchasers of six or more volumes at one time so boxes are also to be found with mixed contents bearing no relation to each other rather than a set of books. This fact is confirmed by advertisements seen in books published around 1800. It was an age in which many charming and dainty books for children were being turned out despite the fulminations of Mrs Sarah Trimmer and her grim and puritanical *Guardian of Education*, 1802-6.

Of course, some pretty poor stuff was published too by the Lumsdens and others, indifferently printed, with wretched badly inked woodcuts: such were Lumsden's chapbooks; and such was Lumsden's *The Merry Cobler* (No. 101), costing 2 d. and so not at all in the lowest grade. The buyers of Lumsden's juveniles seem not to have been very critical in these matters for *The Merry Cobler* itself seems to have been a very good seller, but one is left wondering whether the general standard, along with the prices for many of the books, did not appeal to the Scottish market. That to some extent might account for the very small output of Lumsden books over half a century, although it would seem that books were only a minimal part of their turnover as general stationers.

Generally speaking, however, the standard of Lumsden juveniles was a high one, well up to that of contemporary publishers, often higher, even though in contents they are seldom very original, much of their material, if not also their titles, being taken from earlier publishers. Well-known nursery tales and poems such as *Ali Baba, John Gilpin, Robinson Crusoe,* the lesser known titles being frequently brimming with attempts to combine pleasure with moral instruction (*Goody Two-Shoes,* which for all its moralising, remains a delightful little story) and, quite revoltingly, *The Story of Little Dick* which would have ended much more satisfactorily had the loathsome boy been treated to a good spanking, instead of suddenly becoming, for no reason even hinted at, an unctuous little do-gooder. Mrs Trimmer's influence is very strong here, though she herself had died in 1810.

This general statement on the standard of Lumsden publications is in no way applicable to the chapbooks which, like all others of their kind, have their own standard, not for one moment to be contrasted with that of the juveniles. A sketch by Lear for a limerick and an etching by Rembrandt are worlds apart, but each is proper for its own purpose. The chapbooks are dealt with in the general note to List 6.

Now after many years of neglect, Lumsdens have become collector's pieces. One used to pay a pound or two for them, but recently a few sold at auction in the London sale rooms have fetched between £30 and £40 apiece, and a recent bookseller's catalogue offered a fine copy of *Tommy Playlove and Jacky Lovebook* at £48. In their own age they seem to have attracted little notice. They certainly never won the popularity of the Newbery, Carnan, Wallis, Marshall, and Harris publications. This may have been due simply to lack of advertising and publicity, but more probably because no attempt was made to find a wider market for them outside Scotland. The northern cities (apart from York, Newcastle-upon-Tyne and one or two others) were more given to the production of chapbooks proper, the halfpenny and penny sort sold in bulk to the chapmen and running stationers. Perhaps the sale of the more expensive Lumsden books at twopence to sixpence, and even in four cases we record at one shilling coloured, proved not to be a very paying line, though why so is not evident as these prices were prevailing elsewhere. It can only suggest that the Scottish public were unwilling to spend more than a penny or so on books for their offspring, and it would in some part account for the occasional appearance on the market of copies in almost immaculate condition, i.e. booksellers' unsold stock. Many of the 2*d.* to 6*d.* books have also survived in reasonable condition despite some obvious use which suggests they were thought to be worth keeping and so carefully preserved. Also anyone who could afford to pay several coppers for a small juvenile book could also probably afford a nursemaid who would handle the book rather than the child. This also applies to juvenile books by other publishers which do turn up in fine condition every now and then. On the other hand surprisingly few copies of the halfpenny and penny books or Chapbooks have survived at all, although why this should apply particularly to Lumsden cannot be explained. Chapbooks and other cheap books issued by such well-known publishers as Rusher, Kendrew, Davison, Keys, Richardson and others have survived in large numbers and until recent years were comparatively common. The sole example of a Lumsden halfpenny book we have been able to locate is a copy of *Familiar Objects described* in the Renier collection (now transferred to the Victoria and Albert Museum).

London seems to have noticed Lumsden & Son scarcely at all, judging by the lack of mention of them in the papers and journals where the Newberys and their fellow publishers advertised regularly, often weekly. And this has continued almost to the present day. Harvey Darton apparently considered that Glasgow was outside his range, *Boase's Modern English Biography* only mentions James senior, the founder of the firm, as the father of James junior. And there is no systematic bibliography; even the two volume edition of Miss St. John's catalogue of the Osborne collection at Toronto Public Library has next to nothing to say on the subject, and the collection is weak in these books. A biography of the Lumsden (Lumsdaine) family, 1889, by one Col. Lumsden makes no mention of a family of that name being 'in trade', he seldom descended below Colonels, though admitted there were many other branches of the family, or other families of that name, of which he knew nothing.

As previously mentioned little information has survived relating to the printing and publishing activities of the Lumsdens. The obituary notice of James Lumsden junior is contained in the *Glasgow Herald* for May 19th, 1856. Born on 13th November, 1778 he was apprenticed to his father and entered the family business in 1799. He was a man of very wide interests and enormous energy. He was Lord Provost of Glasgow in 1843-5, and there were (if the obituary is to be believed) few activities in Glasgow, benevolent, educational, philanthropic, etc. with which he was not intimately concerned. These activities take up a great part of the obituary. His connection with James

Lumsden & Son is hardly mentioned, and the publication of his books for children and chapbooks never. Clearly these activities were regarded as of no importance, not worthy of mention. His son, James the third, was born in 1808; he also became Lord Provost of Glasgow and picked up a knighthood. He died in March, 1879. The family home was at Arden House, Alexandria, Dunbartonshire where both James junior and his son lived.

The following excerpt from David Murray's *Bibliography, Its Scope and Methods* mentions the Lumsdens;

'Lumsden's bawbee and penny pictures were the delight of the rising, and will doubtless be remembered, with a smile and a sigh, by the *risen* generation of early days.' So said Andrew Bell (St. Mungo's Bell) in *Northern Notes and Queries*, i. p. 79. Again he says, James Lumsden's 'name was associated in the youthful mind, with sources of enjoyment, "New'r gifts," holiday presents, small prints and *picter byukes* of every description. What a goodly array he had! Why *every* thing in that line was by "James Lumsden & Son." The latter, in the days we write of, had his house of business in an establishment, up a court in Dunlop Street, with an iron-gated garden. What great ideas we had, as we used to peep through that iron *grille*, of the "Paradise of Dainty Devices" within: The "Crooked Family", the "Bloody Battles (by sea and land) of the Rats and Cats", etc., etc., etc. Oh: *what* a treasury, thought we.'

A record of former Lords Provost of Glasgow states that in addition to publishing chapbooks and prints Lumsden also turned out quantities of the diminutive prints for the 'Lottery Books' with which little Glasgow girls once used to pester 'passers-by' with cries of: 'Dab, dab, dab at the picture-book, yin in every four leaves and four for the prize.' The customer made a dab with a pin, and if he got the right page (with four pictures) he won it, and if not he left his pin behind (and his money!). Needless to say a recent request in the *Glasgow Herald* for any reader who had one of these 'fiendish gambling-devices' preserved to get in touch with me (R.A.B.) produced only a stony silence! It is unlikely a specimen has survived, and there is little doubt that in addition to books and chapbooks the firm produced a very wide range of juvenile ephemera, and it is to be regretted that more information is not available.

The total output, so far discovered, of publications the subject of this bibliography, is about 140 juveniles (including religious and educational books) and some 25 chapbooks, spread over a period beginning shortly after 1790 and ending somewhere between 1840 and 1850. Books of these species published after 1823 are all undated. They were fond of grouping their publications under serial titles and listing the cheaper books in advertisement leaves. So we find lists of halfpenny books at the end of *Familiar Objects described*, 1820 (No. 8), of penny and twopenny books in *Foundation of Learning,* 1805 (No. 9). Books with serial titles are dealt with on page 127, where the purpose and fitness of several of the 'titles' is queried.

The firm also put out some single sheets designed, presumably, to decorate the nursery. Only three of these have been located so far, two in the possession of Mr and Mrs Peter Opie and one in Sotheby's catalogue sale of March 4th, 1977, lot 580. The indications suggest that very few of these were published as we have not seen them advertised in any of their publications, though one would assume the expectation of life of such frail little pieces of ephemera as these to be short. It seems highly likely that the firm would also have published *Battledores,* surely a lucrative form of publication, but none has come to light, and it also seems likely that more items of an educational nature remain to be discovered. They also published various local guides, almanacks, tide tables, steamboat companions, a facsimile of Burns' *Jolly Beggars,* and facsimile prints, 'My Grandmother' (a copy in the John Johnson collection at Bodley), 'The Plough Boy' and probably others; all these books and prints being published in the years 1820-50. Other items include *Journal of a Trip to the Algerine Territory* in 1817 by William Lumsden, and a large illuminated edition of *The Pilgrim's Progress* in or about 1860. The latter is the only item to come to light definitely published after 1850, which seems rather strange.

Clearly printing and publishing was only a small part of the Lumsden business. They were primarily stationers, though there is little enough evidence as to what, in the way of stationery they dealt in. The firm was highly thought of in Glasgow, and James senior or junior (the records not being clear on this) was President of the Incorporated Company of Glasgow Stationers in 1815, 1822 and 1830. It is questionable to what extent James junior was actively concerned in the affairs of the firm, absorbed, as he apparently was, in the more exciting activities of Glasgow public life, but this may have been a period which developed after the death of James senior (date unknown) when he would have become head of the firm. It is significant that the firm did not begin to publish books for children on any scale until he joined the firm in 1799 and activity ceased abruptly after his death save for the isolated edition of *The Pilgrim's Progress.* Possibly he was more interested in his share of the profits than anything else, for one would expect the firm to be more concerned that the books it published would attain to the first rank. Had the Lumsdens, both father and son, but especially the son, been really interested in the success of their books, they would surely have exercised some editorial supervision, or have appointed a competent editor, thus removing those abortive attempts to start 'series' of books (see p. 127) which came to nothing, a fault which any business man really concerned would have corrected at once. Although it must be admitted that isolated attempts to enter a better class of market were made, viz. *The New Cries of London* (No. 105) published at 6 *d.* plain or one shilling coloured. There may have been more of these, but this is the only title so far discovered in this price range save for two educational books, *A New History of England* (No. 1a) and *A New History of Scotland* (No. 3). Also it has to be admitted that the quality of many of Lumsden's books indicate some care and typographical skill being exercised in printing and production, but whether this is due to the presence of a general manager of some taste appointed by James junior, or to the hand of James junior himself it is impossible to say. The overall attitude of the firm to its publishing activities remains something of a mystery in the absence of any records.

Walker mentions a Lumsden sale, apparently of books, conducted by James senior (or possibly junior, for here again the records are not clear) in Glasgow. It was then the custom of the 'Southern Publishers' (whatever that may mean) 'to hold their trade sale at the end of a magnificent dinner . . . with after this all the temptations in the shape of the choicest specimens of the finest vintage and the most powerful spirits and liqueurs were presented, when it was naturally expected that the bidding for the books offered, and the articles presented, would be fast and furious'. Walker refers to one of these dubious proceedings as 'Mr. Lumsden's Sale', though apparently the host himself remained 'prudent', as an essential condition if he was to conduct the sale.

As to their book dealings the facts are scanty, though they seem to have been general booksellers as well as publishers. Lumsden senior is described by W. J. Cowper in *The Millers of Haddington*, a record of Scottish booksellers (1914), as a 'prominent bookseller'. The present firm of Glasgow stationers, James Lumsden, Son & Co. has now no connection with the older firm, and has none of the early records: For the facts about their own publications we must turn to the title-page imprints, and these are many and various: 'Published and sold by J. Lumsden & Son', (very frequent), 'Published by J. Lumsden & Son', 'Published and sold wholesale by J. Lumsden & Son' (very frequent), 'Sold by J. Lumsden & Son', 'Printed by . . . and sold wholesale by J. Lumsden & Son', 'Printed by . . . and sold wholesale by J. Lumsden, Engraver', (probably before 1800), 'Printed by . . . for James Lumsden, Engraver', 'Printed and sold by J. Lumsden (once·only, in the 1820 period, omitting the '& Son'). It is a confused record,* showing them sometimes as wholesalers only, sometimes as sellers retail and wholesale, occasionally as sellers only (whether wholesale or retail is not made clear), and once or twice in an unstated capacity. It seems hardly credible that in some cases they sold their own publications both wholesale and retail, in others as wholesale only. It is suggested that these imprints must not be taken too literally.

Another difficulty arises over the dating of the books (other than chapbooks), and it is not possible to list them in any assured chronological order. Out of a count of about 140, only twenty are dated on the title-page. These range from 1794 (Boreman's *A Description of above 300 Animals* (No. 4)) to 1823 (*The Story of Little Dick* (No. 124)). After that year none is dated. Only six books have been found that are definitely pre-1800, so it is very unlikely there were more than one or two at the most (if any at all) before 1794. Of the books published after 1800 a certain rough and very approximate grouping is possible, based on the type faces, the illustrations, the use of the long 's' and the short 's' and so on. 1801 to 1808, 1809 to 1815, 1816 to 1830, and finally the 'late printings' where a more modern typeface is used, from 1831 onwards, possibly as late as 1850 or thereabouts. With the chapbooks the reverse applies: out of twenty-five or six of these only five are undated. The rest bear dates 1808 (*The Unfortunate Lovers* (No. 169) altogether an exception, this), and between 1816 and 1822; of these eight are dated 1822.

It will be noticed that the upper cover of a child's book often adds, following the title, 'From Ross's Juvenile Library', followed by Lumsden's imprint, which also appears on the title-page, for example, *Gulliver*, 1815 (No. 45). Ross can be traced in the Edinburgh directories from 1804 to 1818, either as G. & J. Ross, J. Ross or George Ross, always described as printers, and always at an address in the Horse-Wynd, Edinburgh. But the reference to 'Ross's Juvenile Library' indicates that they were, or attempted to be, publishers. And the 1805 edition of Perrault's *Fairy Tales of Past Times* (No. 69) has Ross's name alone on the title-page. Unfortunately the force of this evidence in favour of Ross as printer *and* publisher is weakened by the common text on the

* No explanation can be offered as to the not infrequent 'Sons' in imprints in place of 'Son'. No record elsewhere has been found of other sons of James Lumsden senior.

upper cover of Perrault's book 'From Ross's Juvenile Library', followed by 'Glasgow; Published by J. Lumsden & Son'. And an edition of Watts' *Divine Songs* (No. 37) has two title-pages, one naming Ross as printer and seller, the other stating Lumsden to be the publisher. The evidence seems to point to Ross being ninety-nine per cent printer, but trying once or twice to break through into publishing with the 'Ross's Juvenile Library' series, an edition of *The House that Jack Built* (No. 85) and a few others, and ending up by selling his stock of books of his own printing to Lumsden, who added or substituted their own wrappers.

All the juvenile books seen have been illustrated, but it is not possible to speak with assurance as to the unseen penny and halfpenny books. But it seems likely it would be found that all are illustrated: the one halfpenny book located *Familiar Objects described* (No. 8) has eight woodcuts on as many pages. A few of the chapbooks are not illustrated.

It can be said with certainty that the Lumsdens appreciated the importance of illustration, both in metal and wood, and, in the more expensive sixpenny books the standard of work is high, *Robinson Crusoe* (No. 115), *The Discreet Princess* (No. 61), etc. Not infrequently the illustrations copy Bewick, the figures of the magpie and the rat at pp. 14 and 17 of *Tommy Thumb's Song Book,* 1814 (No. 20), the trumpeting elephant at p. 48 of *Sindbad,* 1819 (No. 121). They made an approach to the great Thomas Bewick himself in the hope of getting him to design and engrave blocks for them. The following letter to Bewick (now in a private collection) tells its own story.

Glasgow, 17 July 1807.

Dr Sir

I received yesterday a Number of cuts and coincides in oppinion with you that the[y] are done in a very superior manner, but the style is vary farr from what I expressed to you, and I am extremly sorry to say are usless for the purpose intended as no person here can do them Justice in printing, even if the[y] could the prices usually paid for Printing ½d Books — would not warrant the care and attention necessary in working them off, when with you I pointed out a small Halfpenny Book (I think the cuts were done from Stevens lecture on Heads) as the Bold style mines were to be done, and were coarser if possible so as any of our printers could give them effect, — however as whats done cannot be now undone proceed no farther 'till I see you which will be in the course of Two or *Three* months at farthest — In the interim I shall forward by Some opportunity these reseived so as you may make them a little opener in the style twould be usless to putt them to press in the Present state as the coarseness of the paper we use would quite destroy them —

Your Boys appears — to me wishing to rival their *great Instructor* instead of rendering their labours essential to a manufacturer of Tom Thumbs — as the specimen sent might answer for any Publication whatever — Compts to your family and believe me to be with respect

Yours &c

James Lumsden Junr.

Mr. Thomas Bewick / Engraver / Newcastle.

Whether James junior (or perhaps his father) did see Bewick again as suggested in the letter is not known; but no Lumsden books with undoubted Bewick work have been seen, and it is almost certain that by this time Bewick would have given such work to his apprentices, and this is confirmed by the reference to 'Your Boys' in the letter above. Bewick was too expensive, one may suppose, and his work too fine for the Glasgow printers to cope with. They could deal with the cuts in the cheaper books, not more than that, though there were engravers on metal capable of producing the fine vignettes and engravings of *Robinson Crusoe* and others of that standard. It is very likely that Lumsden's criticism of Bewick was not well received. By 1807 Bewick had a nation-wide and established reputation, and could afford to say 'take it or leave it; I make no revisions just to suit your market'. He could speak harshly on occasion.

For the most part the more talented craftsmen who worked on wood used the 'engraving' method (cutting on the end-grain of the block), a method introduced and brought to perfection by Bewick, rather than cutting 'on the plank' (the side-grain of the block). One is often reminded of John Bewick; but very similar in manner was the work of R. Austin, several cuts being signed by him (*The Valentine's Gift*, No. 134.). The manner of this cutter, whoever he was, is firm and precise, dry and clear; he has a great fondness for close parallel lines, either black on white or white on black. Clouds are formed by horizontal lines, walls by verticals, all laid close together, as are the curved lines in the spirited cut of the whale at p. 9 of *Sindbad* (No. 121).

Of the engravers on metal who worked for the Lumsdens two stand out; there were others as well, but of no distinction. These two we will refer to as 'Etcher No. I' and 'Etcher No. II.' Etcher No. I is to be distinguished by frequent close cross-hatching and has a lively sense of design (*An Abridgement of the New Testament*, No. 32). There is movement in his work (*Fun upon Fun*, No. 72), but his human figures are only puppets or marionettes.

Etcher No. II, on the other hand, shows some skill in drawing the human figure, see the cuts in *A Selection of Stories* (No. 118), *Mother Goose* (No. 66), and especially *Little Jack* (No. 93). If it was he who produced the vignette on the title-page to *Robinson Crusoe* (No. 115), he was no mean craftsman. But the author of that cut may have been yet another artist. It is possible that Etcher No. II and the woodcutter discussed above were one and the same person. A fair number of illustrations can only be the work of unknown hack-engravers.

In this short essay an attempt has been made, with the aid of the reproductions, to give some idea of the books published by James Lumsden & Son, in the hope, which now seems likely to be realised, that they will come to rank along with the books under the imprints of more famous publishers.

*Frontispiece to No. 130,* The History of Tommy Playlove and Jacky Lovebook, *1819.*

# LIBRARIES, COLLECTORS AND THEIR SYMBOLS

| | |
|---|---|
| Aberdeen | The University of Aberdeen |
| Ball | The late Miss Elizabeth Ball, Indiana, U.S.A. |
| BCE | Bedford College of Education, Bedford (the Hockliffe Collection) |
| Bell | Dr L. G. E. Bell, Southampton |
| BM | British Museum (now the British Library) |
| Bodley | The Bodleian Library, Oxford |
| Brimmell | R. A. Brimmell, Esq., Hastings |
| CUL | Cambridge University Library |
| FlorSUL | Florida State University Library (the Shaw Collection), U.S.A. |
| Freeman | R. Freeman, Esq., London |
| Garrett | Mrs P. Garrett, Hoddesdon, Herts. |
| GlaPL | Glasgow Public Library |
| GlaUL | Glasgow University Library |
| Gross | Bernard Gross, London |
| Harvard | Harvard University Library, U.S.A. |
| Hornel | Hornel Library, Kirkcudbright |
| Hunley | Maxwell Hunley, California |
| Hyde-Parker | Sir Richard Hyde-Parker, Bt., Long Melford, Suffolk |
| John Johnson | The John Johnson Library, Oxford University Press (now in Bodley) |
| MB | Boston Public Library, Boston, Mass., U.S.A. |
| McEdin | The Museum of Childhood, Edinburgh |
| McKell | Collection of the late David McKell, of Ohio, now owned by Ross County (Ohio) Historical Society, U.S.A. |
| McNaughtan | Mrs M. P. O. McNaughtan, Edinburgh |
| MLG | Mitchell Library, Glasgow |
| Moon | Mrs E. M. Moon, Winchester |
| NLSc | National Library of Scotland, Edinburgh |
| NorBM | Bridewell Museum, Norwich |
| OOxM | Miami University, Oxford, U.S.A. |
| Opie | Mrs and Mrs Peter Opie, West Liss, Hants. |
| Oppenheimer | Collection of the late Edgar S. Oppenheimer, N.Y., U.S.A. (now being sold) |
| Osborne | Osborne Collection of Early Children's Books, Toronto Public Library, Toronto, Canada |

| | |
|---|---|
| OUP | Oxford University Press |
| Platt | M. H. Platt, Esq., Edgware, Middlesex |
| PM | The Pierpont Morgan Library, New York, U.S.A. |
| Preston | The Spencer Collection, Harris Public Library, Preston, Lancs. |
| Rankin | K. M. Rankin, Esq., Gourock, Renfrewshire |
| Renier | Mr and Mrs F. G. Renier, London (now in course of transfer to the V & A Museum, London) |
| Ries | The late Ludwig Ries, of New York |
| Roscoe | The late Sydney Roscoe, St. Leonards on Sea, East Sussex |
| Rylands | George Rylands, Esq., O.B.E., M.A., Cambridge |
| St. Andrews | St. Andrews University Library, St. Andrews |
| Schiller | Justin G. Schiller, Esq., New York, U.S.A. |
| Sheffield | Sheffield University Library |
| Shepard | Leslie Shepard, Esq., Blackrock, Co. Dublin, Eire |
| Spielmann | The late Percy Edwin Spielmann |
| Steedman | Robert D. Steedman, Esq., Newcastle upon Tyne |
| Stockham | Peter Stockham, Esq., Elstree, Herts. |
| Stone | The late Wilbur Macey Stone, U.S.A. (collection now dispersed and location unknown) |
| Traylen | C. W. Traylen, Esq., Guildford |
| UCLA | University of California, Los Angeles, U.S.A. |
| V & A | Victoria & Albert Museum (Guy Little collection) |
| Wandsworth | Wandsworth Public Library, London |
| Welch | The late Dr d'Alté A. Welch, Cleveland Heights, Ohio, U.S.A. (collection bequeathed to UCLA by Mrs Welch) |
| Wellcome | The Wellcome Historical Medical Library, London |
| Wood | Miss E. Yale Wood, Wisbech, Cambs. |

# ABBREVIATIONS

Communicated   Indicates information supplied by the owner.

Illustration/Illustrated   Used where there is no information as to whether a cut is on wood or metal.

The location lists at the end of each item are not to be regarded as censuses of holdings.

| | |
|---|---|
| bds | boards |
| *c.* | circa, about |
| d.p.rule | double plain rule |
| d.s.rule | decorative swelled rule |
| edn(s) | edition(s) |
| engvd | engraved |
| engvg | engraving |
| FP, frontis. | frontispiece |
| n.d. | no date |
| p.rule | plain rule |
| p.s.rule | plain swelled rule, tapering rule |
| p. pp. | page, pages |
| P.L. | Public Library |
| sgd. | signed |
| TP | title-page |
| U.L. | University Library |
| vso | verso |
| unsgd | unsigned |
| wct. | woodcut |
| wmk | watermark |

# 1
# HISTORY

**1. HISTORY OF SCOTLAND.** (*c.* 1805). A Twopenny Book, listed in No. 9.

**1a. NEW HISTORY OF ENGLAND, A.** n.d. (*c.* 1810).
Advertised on the back cover of *A New History of Scotland*, No. 3, as TO BE HAD OF / J. LUMSDEN & SON / A NEW HISTORY OF ENGLAND / SAME PRICE, AND PRINTED UNIFORM WITH SCOT / LAND. The rest of the advertisement is largely illegible in the copy in the British Museum, and has been completely worn off the Roscoe copy, but offers halfpenny, penny, twopenny and threepenny books for children.

**2. NEW HISTORY OF SCOTLAND, A.** n.d. (see note below).
Price 2*d.*
A NEW / HISTORY / OF / SCOTLAND; / FROM THE EARLIEST ACCOUNTS. / WITH THE / LIVES OF FERGUS I. FERGUS II. KENNETH / II. ... [3 lines] / [5 lines quote] / ADORNED WITH COPPER PLATES. / GLASGOW: / PRINTED BY FALCONER & WILLISON, / AND SOLD WHOLESALE BY J. LUMSDEN & SONS, / ENGRAVERS. / (PRICE TWO-PENCE.)
The title is on the verso of the front wrapper. In 12's. 24 leaves, the second signed A, the 4th B, first and last leaves paste-downs. Pp. 47. The 2nd, 5th, 8th, 11th, 14th, 17th, 20th and 23rd leaves are orange-red paper, each with a whole-page woodcut on one side, blank on the other. Floral boards.
*An early publication, 1804 or earlier, the Lumsdens describing themselves as 'Engravers', this statement not found in later books.*
100×60 mm. [Renier.]

**3. NEW HISTORY OF SCOTLAND, A.** n.d. (see note below).
Price 6*d.* plain, (?) 1*s.* coloured.
Plate
A NEW / HISTORY / OF / SCOTLAND. / FROM THE EARLIEST ACCOUNTS / TO THE PRESENT TIME. / [p.s.rule] / ADORNED WITH CUTS OF ALL / THE PRINCI-PAL KINGS AND QUEENS. / [p.rule] / [four lines of verse] / [p.rule] / GLASGOW: / PUBLISHED AND SOLD WHOLESALE BY LUMSDEN & SON. / [PRICE SIXPENCE.]
In 12's. [A-D¹²]. 48 leaves. Pp. 96. 27 woodcuts (whole length) of the sovereigns. The great majority of these are copied from the woodcuts in the *Compendious History of England*, J. Newbery, 1758. Little regard is had to the identity of the sovereign in the cut as against the text (e.g. Newbery's Henry I does duty for

A NEW

## HISTORY

OF

# SCOTLAND.

FROM THE EARLIEST ACCOUNTS

## TO THE PRESENT TIME.

ADORNED WITH CUTS OF ALL

*THE PRINCIPAL KINGS AND QUEENS.*

---

IF Heroes Afhes thus to rake we dare;
And cloud their Bliss by telling tales of War,
'Tis to improve their Sons, who thence may learn,
A well fpent Life alone Juſt Praife can earn.

---

GLASGOW:
Publiſhed and sold wholesale by LUMSDEN & SON.
[*Price Sixpence.*]

---

Alexander II). This hardly accords with the assurance on the front wrapper that the book is adorned with correct likenesses of the Kings and Queens.

Probable date *c.* 1810. There is a watermark '809' at D5 in Roscoe copy.

Pinkish wrappers of stiff paper, with text on the upper: THE / HISTORY / OF / SCOTLAND, / ADORNED WITH / CORRECT LIKENESSES / OF THE / DIFFERENT KINGS AND QUEENS / FROM THE / EARLIEST [illegible] / PRICE 6d PLAIN, and [?] 1s. COLOURED. / [p.rule.] PUBLISHED AND SOLD WHOLESALE, BY LUMSDEN & SON / GLASGOW. On the lower, advertisement for *A New History of England* (No. 1a), etc.

101×84 mm. [BM; Roscoe.]

# 2

# NATURAL HISTORY
# & EDUCATIONAL

A

# DESCRIPTION

OF ABOVE

## THREE HUNDRED

# A N I M A L S,

*V I Z.*

BEASTS,           SERPENTS,
BIRDS,             AND
FISHES,          INSECTS.

W I T H

*A particular Account of the Manner of Catching Whales in Greenland.*

Extracted from the best AUTHORS, and adapted to the Use of all Capacities.

*ILLUSTRATED WITH COPPERPLATES.*

Whereon is curiously Engraven every BEAST, BIRD, FISH, SERPENT, and INSECT, described in the whole Book.

---

PSALM L. 10, 11.

*For every Beast of the forest is mine, and the Cattle upon a thousand Hills. I know all the Fowls of the Mountains, and the wild Beasts of the Field are mine.*

---

# G L A S G O W:

*PRINTED FOR JAMES LUMSDEN, ENGRAVER.*

M. DCC. XCIV.

[PRICE THREE SHILLINGS BOUND]

**4. BOREMAN, Thomas. A DESCRIPTION OF ABOVE THREE HUNDRED ANIMALS.** 'Nineteenth edition', 1794. Price 3*s*. Bound.

Plate

A / DESCRIPTION / OF ABOVE / THREE HUNDRED / ANIMALS, / VIZ. / BEASTS, SERPENTS, / BIRDS, AND / FISHES, INSECTS. / [thick and thin central dividing lines between these three lines] / WITH / A PARTICULAR AC-COUNT OF THE MANNER OF / CATCHING WHALES IN GREENLAND. / EXTRACTED FROM THE BEST .AUTHORS, AND ADAPTED TO / THE USE OF ALL CAPACITIES. / ILLUSTRATED WITH COPPERPLATES. / WHEREON IS CURIOUSLY ENGRAVEN EVERY BEAST, BIRD, FISH, / SERPENT, AND INSECT, DESCRIBED IN THE WHOLE BOOK. / [p.rule] / PSALM L. 10, 11. / FOR EVERY BEAST OF THE FOREST IS MINE, AND THE CATTLE UPON A THOUSAND / HILLS. I KNOW ALL THE FOWLS OF THE MOUNTAINS, AND THE WILD BEASTS / OF THE FIELD ARE MINE. / [p.rule] / GLASGOW: / PRINTED FOR JAMES LUMSDEN, ENGRAVER. / M. DCC. XCIV. / [PRICE THREE SHILLINGS BOUND].

Collation and pagination very irregular. 164 leaves. For details see Lisney, who gives a full collation, etc. and records pp. 207. The numerous engraved leaves are included in the pagination and numbered accordingly. The engraved frontis. is a rather free sketch, in reverse, after the frontis. in the 11th edition of 1774 and earlier (reproduced in Roscoe, *Newbery*, No. J41). A few of the engraved figures may derive from Bewick. 166×96 mm. [Sheffield.]

**5. BOREMAN, Thomas. A DESCRIPTION OF ABOVE THREE HUNDRED ANIMALS.** 1796.

A / DESCRIPTION / OF / ABOVE / THREE HUNDRED / ANIMALS. / VIZ: / BEASTS, SERPENTS, BIRDS AND INSECTS. WITH / A PARTICULAR ACCOUNT OF THE MANNER OF / CATCHING WHALES IN GREENLAND. / EXTRACTED FROM THE BEST AUTHORS, AND ADAPTED TO THE / USE OF ALL CAPACITIES. / ILLUS-TRATED WITH COPPERPLATES. / WHEREON IS CURI-OUSLY ENGRAVED EVERY BEAST, BIRD, FISH, SER-PENT, / AND INSECT DESCRIBED IN THE WHOLE BOOK. / [p.rule] / [3 lines quote] / [p.rule] / [p.s.rule] / PAISLEY: / PRINTED BY J. NEILSON, / FOR JAMES

LUMSDEN, ENGRAVER, GLASGOW. / [d.p.rule] / M.DCC.XCVI.
Irregular format. Engraved frontis. and numerous full-page engravings. Pp. [4], 207. A few of the engraved leaves copied after, or deriving from, Bewick. The text follows the Bewick edition.
168×98 mm. [Freeman.]

**6. BOREMAN, Thomas. HISTORY OF THE 300 ANIMALS.**
An edition so described is listed in *The History of Elspy Campbell*, 1799 (No. 57). Very probably No. 5, the 1796 edition.

THE
## CHILD'S INSTRUCTOR,
OR
*Picture Alphabet.*

Good Girls and good Boys
Prefer Books to Toys,
And with the Cock rise
To read and grow wise.

GLASGOW,
PUBLISHED AND SOLD, WHOLESALE, BY
*LUMSDEN & SON.*

Price TWOPENCE.

A a

An-gler.                    *An-gler.*

ab   eb   ib   ob   ub

An An-gler is one who catch-es fish-es with a hook.

**7. CHILD'S INSTRUCTOR, THE.** n.d. (see note below). Price 2*d.* Hugo 313.
Plate
THE / CHILD'S INSTRUCTOR, / OR / PICTURE AL-PHABET. / [oval woodcut] / [4 lines of verse] / [p.s.rule] / GLASGOW, / PUBLISHED AND SOLD, WHOLESALE, BY /

LUMSDEN & SON. / [wavy rule] / PRICE TWOPENCE.
The title-page is printed either on the verso of the front wrapper or on the verso of the first free leaf.
A single gathering of 14 or 16 leaves, unsigned and un-numbered. 27 small oval woodcuts, several of which are used in other Lumsden publications, e.g. the farmyard cock in the title-page used at p. 3 of *Gammer Gurton's Garland* (No. 17), the squirrel at p. 26. The alphabet woodcuts of birds and animals for the letters E, G, J, K, and S are copied after Bewick. On the last page is a woodcut of a Stanhope printing press, the device of HEDDERWICK / PRINTER GLASGOW.
The watermark date in the last free leaf in a copy in the Roscoe collection seems to be '181–', but the last figure is not legible. It may be 1812 or 1819.
Most copies are in plain wrappers, drab, pink, brown, blue, blue-grey. The BM copy in pink wrappers has on the front wrapper, a woodcut of a stout physician with text 'I FEEL YOUR PULSE & TAKE YOUR FEE / TO DIE YOU'R THEN AT LIBERTY', and on the back wrapper a woodcut of a very obese magistrate, with text 'THIS WORTHY MAGISTRATE THEY SAY / TAKES HIS THREE GALL$^{NS}$ EVERY DAY'. The CUL copy, in grey-blue wrappers, has a woodcut, 'QUEEN JOSEPHINE' on front, & 'EMPEROR NAPPY' on back.
*Hugo says 'With 27 very pretty oval cuts, some of them, as that of the Weathercock above the Exchange at Newcastle with the Steeple of St. Nicholas in the distance, clearly by Thomas Bewick.' The most that can be said is that some of the woodcuts are copied after him or produced under his influence, and may have been done in his workshop. The Weathercock cut referred to by Hugo is the feeblest thing in the book. The cuts of 'Drunkard', 'Inn', 'Melon', 'Rain-bow', 'U-sur-er' cannot, by any stretch of the imagination, be described as 'pretty'.*
103×67 mm. [Aberdeen; BCE; Bell; Bodley; BM; CUL; Garrett; GlaUL (3 copies); Hornel; MB; NLSc; Osborne; OUP; Rankin; Renier; Roscoe (2 copies); Steedman (Cat. 78); V & A; Welch.]


**8. FAMILIAR OBJECTS DESCRIBED.** n.d. (*c.* 1820). Price $\frac{1}{2}d$.
FAMILIAR OBJECTS DESCRIBED. / [wavy rule] / [rectangular woodcut] / [wavy rule] / GLASGOW: / JAMES LUMSDEN AND SON. / [p.rule] / PRICE ONE HALFPENNY.
A single gathering of 8 unsigned leaves. Pp. 14,5 (error for 15). 8 woodcuts including one on the back wrapper, has a list of the Halfpenny Books: *House that Jack Built*; *Toby Tickle's Puzzling-*

*Cap*; *History of Whittington and his Cat*; *William and his Little Dog*; *History of Henry Robinson*; *Amusing Riddle Book*; *Giles Gingerbread*; *Juvenile Learner*; *History of Peter Martin*; *Familiar Objects described*; *Babes in the Wood*; *Three Travelling Cocks.*
Yellow wrappers.
100×62 mm. [Renier.]

**9. FOUNDATION OF LEARNING, THE.** n.d. (*c.* 1805). Price 1*d.*
THE / FOUNDATION / OF / LEARNING; / AND GROUND WORK OF / KNOWLEDGE; / OR, THE / ALPHABET / IN DIFFERENT CHARACTERS. / ADORNED WITH COPPERPLATES. / [d.p.rule] / GLASGOW, / PUBLISHED AND SOLD WHOLESALE BY / J. LUMSDEN AND SON, / AT THEIR TOY-BOOK MANUFACTORY. / (PRICE ONE PENNY).
Pp. 8,[23] (most pp. un-numbered). Woodcut pictorial alphabet. List of penny and twopenny books published and sold by J. Lumsden & Son at p. [23]. Penny Books: *Foundation of Learning*; *Robinson Crusoe*; *Holy Bible*; *Testament and Psalms*; *Mr. Jacky and Miss Harriot*; *Little Red Riding Hood*; *History of Elspy Campbell*; *Songsters of the Grove*; *Watts' Divine Songs*; *Tom Thumb's Play Book*; *History of Giles Gingerbread*; *Babes in the Wood*; *Whittington and his Cat*; *Tommy Trip's Valentine Gift.* Twopenny Books: *King Pippin*; *New Testament*; *History of Scotland*; *Merry Andrew*; *Watts' Divine Songs*; *Wonders of a Day.*
Wrappers, the lower has a woodcut and verses.
104×63 mm. [OOxM.]

**10. JUVENILE LEARNER, THE.** n.d. (*c.* 1830-40). Price 1*d.*
TP on recto of front wrapper: LUMSDEN AND SON'S SUPERIOR EDITION OF PENNY BOOKS. / [p.rule] / THE / JUVENILE LEARNER; / OR, THE / CHILD'S / EARLY GUIDE. / [Woodcut] / [p.rule] / GLASGOW: / PUBLISHED BY LUMSDEN & SON. [The whole within an ornamental frame.]
6 unsigned leaves, inclusive of the wrappers. Pp. 11. 5 woodcuts in text, flanked by printer's ornaments.
Buff wrappers; the legend on the back wrapper THE / JUVENILE LEARNER; etc. as for the front, but with a different woodcut. [The whole within an ornamental frame.]
129×77 mm. [BM.]

**11. JUVENILE LEARNER, THE.** (*c.* 1820). A Halfpenny Book listed in No. 8.

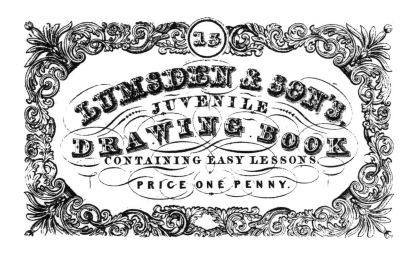

**12. LUMSDEN & SON'S JUVENILE DRAWING BOOK CONTAINING EASY LESSONS.** n.d. Price 1*d.* each.
Plate
LUMSDEN & SON'S / JUVENILE / DRAWING BOOK / CONTAINING EASY LESSONS / PRICE ONE PENNY. [The whole surrounded by a decorative border with the number of the booklet at the top in a circle. In some cases this is repeated on the lower cover but of 8 copies examined 6 had lower cover left blank.]
Various numbers up to 13 have been traced of this series but it is not possible to say what constitutes a complete set. Numbers located are: 3, 4, 5, 7, 8, 10, 11, 12 and 13.
Each issue consists of the TP and 4 etchings, of considerable merit being of the soft-ground variety. There is no text apart from the title-page. Details of contents as follows: No. 3. Tower of London and other landscapes with buildings; 4. Rustic scenes with cottages or other buildings; 5. Cottage and parkland scenes; 7. Horses; 8. Dogs and Sheep; 10. Domestic fowls; 11. Reflections of buildings, etc. in water; 12. Figures and heads including a boy with a cricket bat; 13. Boy's games.
The 'Easy Lessons' in the title-page must indicate that the etchings were to be copied. Oblong, sewed. Paper wrappers

either yellow or blue. Can be dated anywhere between 1820 and 1850.

*c.* 80×126 mm. [Nos. 3, 5, 7, 8, 10, 11, 12, 13: Brimmell. Nos. 4 and 13: John Johnson.]

**13. NATURAL HISTORY OF BEASTS AND BIRDS.** n.d. (1830-40). Price 2*d.*
NATURAL HISTORY / OF / BEAST AND BIRDS. / [p.rule] / EMBELLISHED WITH / BEAUTIFUL COLOURED PLATES. / [p.rule] / GLASGOW: / PUBLISHED BY J. LUMSDEN & SON. [The whole within a ruled surround.]
The title reads 'Beast' instead of Beasts (as on covers).
A single gathering of 12 leaves. Title-page, [verso blank], [5], 6, [7-8], 9-12, [13-16], 17-20, [21-22], 23-26. Pp. 26[28]. The wrappers are included in reckoning the pagination, but, with the leaves of plates, are not numbered. The FP is on the verso of the upper wrapper, which bears the text LUMSDEN & SON'S / IMPROVED EDITION / OF / COLOURED / TWOPENNY BOOKS. . . . The lower wrapper advertises Lumsden as sellers of coloured prints and maps. There are coloured engraved illustrations in the text (2 to the page), blank on the reverse. Wrappers, pale green-grey lettered in black.
120×80 mm. [Rylands.]

**14. PICTURE ALPHABET.** Included in Lot 195 of the Edwin Pearson Sale Catalogue, 1868. Alphabets with illustrative pictures were common enough in this period, following the admirable example of Comenius. See *The Child's Instructor* (No. 7), *The Merry Cobbler* (No. 101), *The Rise of Learning* (No. 16).

**15. READING MADE QUITE EASY AND DIVERTING.** By Tom Thumb. 1846.
READING / MADE / QUITE EASY AND DIVERTING; / CONTAINING / SYMBOLICAL CUTS FOR THE AL-PHABET; TABLES OF WORDS OF ONE, TWO, / THREE, AND FOUR SYLLABLES; WITH EASY LESSONS FROM THE SCRIP- / TURES, AT THE END OF EACH TABLE, NOT EXCEEDING THE ORDER OF / SYLLABLES IN THE FOREGOING TABLES; INSTRUCTIVE FABLES, AND / EDIFYING PIECES OF POETRY, WITH SONGS, MORAL AND DIVINE, FROM / I. WATTS. / METHODICALLY DIGESTED; AND CALCULATED, AFTER THE MANNER PRE- / SCRIBED BY THE GREAT MR. LOCKE, TO GAIN

THE ATTENTION OF CHIL- / DREN; WHO BEING
COZENED, OR CHEATED INTO A LOVE OF LEARNING, /
BY THE HUMOUR OF THE NARRATION, ARE ALMOST
INSENSIBLY LED ON / TO READ THE LONGEST WORDS
WITH EASE AND PLEASURE. / TO WHICH IS ADDED, /
THE CHURCH CATECHISM; / WITH SEVERAL ENTER-
TAINING STORIES, PROVERBS, MORAL / SAYINGS,
RIDDLES, &c., / AND CURIOUS ALPHABETICAL GIM-
CRACKS. / [p.rule] / A NEW EDITION, / NEW MODELLED,
GREATLY ENLARGED, AND IMPROVED. / [p.rule] / BY
TOM THUMB, A LOVER OF CHILDREN, / W. WIELD, AND
OTHERS. / [p.rule] / GLASGOW: / PRINTED BY JAMES
LUMSDEN AND SON, / FOR / JOHN SINCLAIR, JOHN
ANDERSON, ALLAN ANDERSON, / JOHN M'KINNELL,
AND J. C. MONTGOMERY & CO. / BOOKSELLERS, DUM-
FRIES. / 1846.
$A^{12}$, $B^8$, $C^{12}$, $D^8$, $E^{12}$, $F^8$, $G^{12}$, $H^6$. Paginated from p. 1 to p. 156.
With frontispiece and 4 pp. of alphabet pictures [pp. 7-10].
Binding quarter dark roan with orange paste paper sides,
probably original.
(Communicated.)
130×85 mm. [NLSc.]

**16. RISE OF LEARNING, THE.** By 'Mrs. Winlove'. n.d. Price
2*d*.
THE / RISE OF LEARNING, / OR / GROUND-WORK OF
SCIENCE. / SHEWING HOW / GOOD BOYS AND GIRLS /
BY ATTENDING TO THE RULES CONTAINED IN / THIS
BOOK / AND OBEYING THEIR PARENTS / AND GUAR-
DIANS, MAY ACQUIRE WISDOM, RICHES, AND HON-
OUR. / BY MRS. WINLOVE. / [rule] / GLASGOW. / PUB-
LISHED BY J. LUMSDEN & SON / [rule] / PRICE TWO
PENCE.
In 8's. [A-$C^8$]. Pp. 7-47. First and last leaves paste-downs.
*A book of instruction for children, with illustrative pictures, easy*
*lessons, fables, etc. The identity of Mrs. Winlove is not known. 'Solomon*
*Winlove' wrote* Moral Lectures *and* Approved Stories *for Newbery.*
(Communicated.)
96×60 mm. [GlaPL; MB.]

# 3
# SONGS

**17. GAMMER GURTON'S GARLAND OF NURSERY SONGS.** n.d. (see note below). Price 2 *d.* Hugo 315. Opie, *Nursery Rhymes*, p. xxvi.
Plate

GAMMER GURTON's

GARLAND OF

NURSERY SONGS,

AND

*TOBY TICKLE'S'*

Collection of

RIDDLES.

Compiled by

*PETER PUZZLECAP, Esq.*

Embellished with a variety of Cuts.

Glasgow:

*Published and Sold Wholesale,*

BY LUMSDEN AND SON.

[Price Twopence.]

GAMMER GURTON'S / GARLAND OF / NURSERY SONGS, / AND / TOBY TICKLE'S / COLLECTION OF / RIDDLES. / [p.rule] / COMPILED BY / PETER PUZZLECAP, ESQ. / [p.rule] / EMBELLISHED WITH A VARIETY OF CUTS. / [p.rule] [p.s.rule] / GLASGOW: / PUBLISHED AND SOLD WHOLESALE, / BY LUMSDEN AND SON. / [PRICE TWOPENCE.]
A single gathering of 16 leaves, the 5th signed B. Pp. 32. 26 small oval or rectangular woodcuts, some in the manner of the Bewick school or copied after figures in the *Quadrupeds* and *Birds* (e.g. at pp. 21, 24, 26). But Hugo's statement 'with 28 charming cuts by

Thomas Bewick' cannot be justified (consider the cuts at pp. 2, 4, 15 and 31).
Can be dated 1815-20.
Wrappers — yellow, blue, pink, drab. In some cases the wrappers are without text or woodcuts; in others there are large bold cuts of 'Queen Josephine', 'Emperor Nappy', 'Darby and his wife Joan', 'The Cobbler in his Stall', 'Punch and Judy', and so on. See Plate.
*Like* Fun upon Fun *this seems to have been a most popular production. Another* Gammer Gurton *was published by R. Triphook about the same time, but with entirely different contents. (See NBL No. 327.)*
102×66 mm. [Aberdeen; Bell; BM; Bodley (2 copies); GlaPL; GlaUL (4 copies); MB; NLSc; Rankin; Roscoe (2 copies); Steedman (Cat. 1978); V & A (2 copies).]


**18. LITTLE WARBLER, THE.**
Vols. I-III and V only have been traced, one copy of each. Possible dates: Vols. I-III in the 1815-20 period; Vol. V would no doubt be the same. The high quality of the engravings and the type used point to this period; the short 's' is used; the long 's' was still being used in Lumsden's Juvenilia in 1814. The price of Vol. V was 6*d.*, for the others presumably the same. Vols. I-III in Mr Leslie Shepard's collection are bound in one, recent brown morocco.

Vol. I. SCOTTISH SONGS.
[? a blank] / *engraved* FP / *engraved* TP: THE / LITTLE WARBLER / SCOTTISH SONGS / [Vignette] / PUBLISHED BY / LUMSDEN & SON / GLASGOW / *printed* TP: IMPROVED EDITION / OF THE / LITTLE WARBLER, / BEING A / SELECTION / OF THE MOST / POPULAR AND ESTEEMED / SCOTCH, ENGLISH, AND IRISH / SONGS. / [wavy rule] / Vol. I. / SCOTTISH SONGS. / [wavy rule] / GLASGOW: / PUBLISHED BY JAMES LUMSDEN & SON, / QUEEN STREET.
At the foot of the last page A. & J. M. DUNCAN, PRINTERS, GLASGOW.
In 12's. [A-F¹²]. 71 or 72 leaves+2 engraved insets. Pp. 136[140]. 71+40 mm. [Shepard.]

Vol. II. ENGLISH SONGS.
[? a blank] / *engraved* FP 'T. Lane del H. Adlard sculp' / *engraved* TP: THE / LITTLE WARBLER / ENGLISH SONGS /

[vignette] / PUBLISHED BY / LUMSDEN & SON / GLASGOW / *printed* TP: as for Vol. I, except Vol. II / ENGLISH SONGS. At the foot of the last page A. & J. M. DUNCAN, PRINTER, GLASGOW.
In 12's. [A-F¹²]. 71 or 72 leaves+2 engraved insets. Pp. 136[141].
71×40 mm. [Shepard.]


Vol. III. IRISH SONGS.
[? a blank] / *engraved* FP: 'T. Lane delt H. Adlard sculp' *engraved* TP: THE / LITTLE WARBLER / IRISH SONGS / [vignette] (with text 'Souse to the bottom just like a blind pup') / PUBLISHED BY / LUMSDEN & SON / GLASGOW / *printed* TP as for Vol. I. except Vol. III / IRISH SONGS.
In 12's. [A-F¹²], last leaf a blank. 71 or 72 leaves+2 engraved insets. Pp. 136[140].
71×40 mm. [Shepard.]


Vol. IV not traced.


Vol V. SCOTTISH COMIC SONGS.
THE LITTLE WARBLER. / SCOTTISH COMIC SONGS. / [Large vignette showing a thistle, comic mask, an open music book and a horn.] / PUBLISHED BY / LUMSDEN & SON / GLASGOW.
Engraved frontis. entitled 'The Turnimspike'. Engraved title-page. 136 pp. Printed wrappers lettered 'The LITTLE WAR-BLER'. Vol. V. Price 6*d*.
*Originally published by T. Oliver in Edinburgh, 1803.*
71×38 mm. [Spielmann.]


**18a. MINIATURE MELODIST, THE.** n.d. (*c.* 1830).
Engraved title and frontispiece, printed title-page. Binding, calf, with black end-papers.
*A collection of largely Scottish lyrics. Not listed in Spielmann catalogue.*
(Communicated.)
69×44 mm. [David Bristow Antiquarian Booksellers (Cat. 1979).]


**19. SONGSTERS OF THE GROVE.** (*c.* 1805). A Penny Book, listed in No. 9.

TOMMY THUMB'S
*SONG-BOOK,*
FOR ALL LITTLE
MASTERS AND MISSES.
To be Sung to them by their Nurfes till
they can fing them themfelves.

BY NURSE LOVECHILD.

To which is prefixed
*A Letter from a Lady on Nursing.*

GLASGOW :
Published by
J. LUMSDEN & SON.

1814.

*Every pretty Moral Tale*
*Shall o'er the Infant Mind prevail.*

**20. TOMMY THUMB'S SONG-BOOK.** 1814. Price 2*d*.
Plate
TOMMY THUMB'S / SONG-BOOK, / FOR ALL LITTLE /
MASTERS AND MISSES. / TO BE SUNG TO THEM BY
THEIR NURSES TILL / THEY CAN SING THEM THEM-
SELVES. / [p.rule] / BY NURSE LOVECHILD / [p.rule] / TO
WHICH IS PREFIXED / A LETTER FROM A LADY ON
NURSING. / [d.p.rule] / GLASGOW: / PUBLISHED BY / J.
LUMSDEN & SON. / [p.rule] / 1814.
16 unsigned leaves, first and last paste-downs. Pp. 31. Woodcut
frontis. and 27 other woodcuts, those at pp. 9-17 being 2 to the
page. The woodcuts of the Magpie and the Rat at pp. 14 and 17
are copied after Bewick.
Wrappers: yellow green, blue, grey-blue. On front wrapper
PRICE TWOPENCE. / FROM / ROSS'S / JUVENILE /
LIBRARY. within an ornamental frame, followed by Lumsden's
imprint. On back wrapper of some copies a reversible head.

101×63 mm. [Bodley; GlaUL (2 copies); Hyde-Parker; MB; Steedman (Cat. 1978); V & A.]

**21. TOMMY THUMB'S SONG-BOOK.** 1815. Price 2*d.* (See the Pierpont Morgan Cat. of Children's Literature, 1954, Item 175. N.B.L. No. 328, which erroneously describes it as the 1st edition.)

Except for the date, the title is as for the edition of 1814, the woodcuts, with one exception, repeated. The type has been reset.

Wrappers, yellow, drab, grey-green, blue, dark green. The legend on the upper wrapper is, except for the frame, as for the 1814 edition. On the lower wrapper is either a reversible head or, in some cases, another woodcut (in the Roscoe copy an old woman carrying a sack, in an oval frame).

104×65 mm. [Aberdeen; BM; Bodley; GlaPL; GlaUL; MLG; Opie; Oppenheimer; Rankin; Roscoe; Sotheby, 6 February 1945; V & A.]

**22. VICISSITUDE: OR THE LIFE AND ADVENTURES OF NED FROLIC.** 1818. Price not stated, probably 6*d.*

Plate

VICISSITUDE: / OR THE LIFE AND ADVENTURES / OF / NED FROLIC. / [p.s.rule] / AN ORIGINAL / COMIC SONG. / [p.s.rule] / FOR THE ENTERTAINMENT OF / ALL GOOD BOYS AND GIRLS / IN THE / BRITISH EMPIRE. / [thick and thin rule] / GLASGOW: / PUBLISHED AND SOLD BY J. LUMSDEN & SON. / 1818. / [p.rule] / NIVEN, PRINTER.

A single gathering of 8 leaves of text, [A⁸], +4 leaves of whole page etchings, hand-coloured, blank on verso, the first forming the FP. Pp. 16. The etched leaves are not reckoned in the pagination.

Stiff paper wrappers, cream, blue-green, pale pink. No label.

*A Drinking Song of 23 verses, harmless, but scarcely appropriate for young ears. The chorus is repeated at the end of each verse: 'So then to be cheerful and happy, / And end the fatigues of the day, / A jorum I take of brown nappy, / Which makes me quite jocund and gay'.*

138×87 mm. [BCE; CUL; Elkin Mathews (Cat. 163); GlaUL; McNaughtan; MLG; Osborne; Roscoe (2 copies); Schiller; Welch.]

# VICISSITUDE:

### OR THE

### LIFE AND ADVENTURES

#### OF

# NED FROLIC.

### AN ORIGINAL

## *COMIC SONG.*

For the Entertainment of

### ALL GOOD BOYS AND GIRLS

#### IN THE

### British Empire.

### GLASGOW:

#### PUBLISHED AND SOLD BY J. LUMSDEN & SON.

#### 1818.

*Niven, Printer.*

**WATTS' DIVINE SONGS.** See List 4, Nos. 34-40.

# 4

# RELIGIOUS WORKS
# & WATTS' HYMNS

Frontispeice.

ADAM & EVE.

*reduced*

# AN ABRIDGEMENT OF THE HOLY BIBLE

Embellished with Elegant Engravings.

GLASGOW.
Published and Sold Wholesale by
LUMSDEN and SON
PRICE SIXPENCE.

**23. ABRIDGEMENT OF THE HISTORY OF THE HOLY BIBLE, AN.** n.d. (not after 1801, see note below). Price 1*d.*
AN / ABRIDGEMENT / OF THE / HISTORY / OF THE / HOLY BIBLE. / ADORNED WITH COPPERPLATES. / [p.rule] / [4 lines verse] / [p.rule] / [decorative rule] / GLASGOW: / PRINTED BY J. & A. DUNCAN, / AND SOLD WHOLESALE BY J. LUMSDEN, / ENGRAVER, GLASGOW. / [PRICE ONE PENNY.]
A single gathering of 12 leaves, the second signed B. Pp. 22,2 (error for 23). Four leaves of etchings in sanguine, two scenes to each leaf; these leaves are integral in the gathering, but unnumbered. Three woodcuts in the text.
Describing Lumsden as 'Engraver' indicates an early publication, very possibly before the turn of the century. The Wandsworth copy has a dated inscription on page 9 'James Forshaw His Book 1801'.
Wrappers, of the same paper as the text, with reversible heads on front and back.
101×61 mm. [Wandsworth.]

**24. ABRIDGEMENT OF THE HISTORY OF THE HOLY BIBLE, AN.** n.d. (*c.* 1805). Price 1*d.*
AN / ABRIDGEMENT / OF THE / HISTORY / OF THE / HOLY BIBLE. / [p.s.rule] / ADORNED WITH COPPER-PLATES. / [p.rule] / [4 lines verses] / [p.rule] / GLASGOW: / PUBLISHED AND SOLD WHOLESALE BY / J. LUMSDEN & SON, / AT THEIR TOYBOOK MANUFACTORY. / [PRICE ONE PENNY.]
Pp. 23. Engraved leaves. Printed and 'illustrated' red paper wrappers.
*This may well be the* HOLY BIBLE *(price 1*d.*) listed in* Foundations of Learning *(No. 9, c. 1805).*
(Communicated.)
100 mm. [OOxM.]

**25. ABRIDGEMENT OF THE HOLY BIBLE, AN.** n.d. (*c.* 1820). Price 6*d.*
Plate
AN [with decorative scroll surround] / ABRIDGEMENT [with decorative scroll surround] / OF THE / HOLY BIBLE [with decorative scroll surround] / [p.rule] / EMBELLISHED WITH ELEGANT / ENGRAVINGS. / [woodcut Noah's Ark] / GLASGOW. / PUBLISHED AND SOLD WHOLESALE BY / LUMSDEN AND SON / PRICE SIXPENCE. / [p.rule].

Format uncertain. [A B⁵ C]. [16 leaves] 24 leaves + engraved FP and TP and 6 other engraved leaves in text. Pp. 60, the engraved leaves reckoned in the pagination. Small wcts at pp. 17, 52, 60. 108×77 mm. [CUL.]

**26. BIBLE IN MINIATURE, THE.** n.d. (not before 1813, see note below). Roscoe: Bibles, No. 45.
Plate
THE / BIBLE / IN / MINIATURE, / INTENDED AS A / PRESENT / FOR / YOUTH. / [p.rule] / SOLD BY / LUMSDEN AND SON. [The whole within a rectangular frame of thick single rules.]
Divisional title to New Testament, at p. 141: A / CONCISE HISTORY / OF THE / NEW TESTAMENT. / [p.rule] / SOLD BY / LUMSDEN AND SON. [The whole within rectangular frame of thick single rules.]
In 8's. [A-O⁸ P-Q⁴]. 120 leaves. Pp. 240. 10 woodcuts averaging 28×25 mm., within frames of single rules. Late Dutch flowered boards without gilt.
There are many dates in the watermarks, unfortunately very difficult to interpret. The earliest date in the Roscoe copy appears to be 1813.
42×35 mm. [Bondy (Cat. 79); Roscoe; Stone.]

**27. CURIOUS HIEROGLYPHIC BIBLE, A.** 24th edition. n.d. (c. 1815-20). Price 1s.
A CURIOUS / HIEROGLYPHIC BIBLE; / OR, / SELECT PASSAGES / IN THE / OLD AND NEW TESTAMENTS. / INTERSPERSED WITH / EMBLEMATICAL FIGURES, / FOR THE / AMUSEMENT OF YOUTH: / DESIGNED CHIEFLY / TO FAMILIARIZE TENDER AGE, IN A PLEASING AND / DIVERTING MANNER, WITH EARLY IDEAS OF / THE HOLY SCRIPTURES. / [p.rule] / THE

TWENTY-FOURTH EDITION. / [p.rule] / GLASGOW: / PRINTED AND SOLD BY J. LUMSDEN. / [p.rule] / PRICE ONE SHILLING.

Pp. 107. Woodcut FP and many cuts in the text. Buff paper wrappers, with text and illustrations (? wcts) 'Christ healing the sick' and 'Peter and Andrew caught', within an ornamental frame on front wrapper; list of 'Books for Children, printed by J. Bailey, 116, Chancery Lane, London' on back.

*'The Twenty-fourth Edition' would seem to be a puff. It is certainly not the 24th of any edition published by Lumsden, and has different text and woodcuts from any other edition seen. It is unknown to Clouston, who knew of none such published in Scotland; Oliver & Boyd did one in 1818.*

*Very notable is the imprint 'Printed and sold by J. Lumsden' omitting the '& Son'. For another imprint similar in this respect one must go back to the* History of Master Jackey & Miss Harriot *of the pre-1800 period (No. 99). No copy of the book examined, only Xerox copies of selected leaves; but there is nothing to suggest the book was published before c. 1815, or a little later. The absence of '& Son' remains unexplained.*

*Bailey's list of books for Children on the back wrapper comprises:* Reading made easy, or Children's Primer, 4d.; Reading made easy, or Children's Spelling Book, *(? 6d.)*; The Child's Picture Book, 2d.; Dr. Watts' Hymns for Children, 3d.; Gray's Elegy, 6d.; Fenelon's Pious Reflections, 6d.; The Economy of Human Life, *(? 1s. 6d.)*; Ali Baba, 6d.; Heathen Mythology, in verse. *(? 1s. 6d.)*; Laws of the Game of Cricket. 4d. *The late Mr Ludwig Ries, the owner of the only copy traced of this edition, assured me the list was printed on the wrapper, not on a pasted-on label. The Osborne catalogue records that Bailey fl. 1810. A Chapbook* The Unfortunate Lovers *(No. 169) was published under the imprint of Bailey & Lumsden in 1808, but it is not clear whether Lumsden was publisher and seller, or only the latter (which seems more probable).*

135 mm. [Ries.]

**28. HISTORY OF THE BIBLE WITH 48 COPPER-CUTS.** (*c.* 1799). Price 8*d.* Listed in No. 64.

**29. HISTORY OF THE HOLY BIBLE ABRIDGED.** n.d. (*c.* 1805). Price 6*d.*

*Engraved TP*: THE / HISTORY / OF THE / HOLY BIBLE / ABRIDGED / [d.p.rule] / EMBELLISHED WITH EIGHT ELEGANT / COPPER PLATE PRINTS / [d.p.rule] / vignette, the Fiery Serpent set on a pole, *Numbers* 21, 8-9] / GLASGOW /

PUBLISHED BY LUMSDEN & SON AT THEIR / TOY BOOK MANUFACTORY / PRICE SIXPENCE.
Pp. 52. Engraved FP and 6 other engraved leaves. Marbled bds, entraved label on upper cover LUMSDEN & SONS. / CHILDRENS LIBRARY / HISTORY OF THE / BIBLE. [Within an oval ornamental frame.]
(Communicated.)
[Ries; Sotheby, 16 March 1970, lot 218.]

**30. HOLY BIBLE.** (*c.* 1805). A Penny Book, listed in No. 9. This is probably No. 24.

**31. NEW TESTAMENT.** (*c.* 1805). A Twopenny Book, listed in No. 9. A twopenny *New Testament* was listed in *Elspy Campbell,* 1799 (No. 64).

**32. NEW TESTAMENT. AN ABRIDGEMENT.** n.d. Price 2*d.* Plate
AN ABRIDGEMENT / OF THE / NEW TESTAMENT; / OR,

THE / LIFE, / MIRACLES, AND DEATH, / OF / OUR LORD & SAVIOUR / JESUS CHRIST. / [p.rule] / EMBELLISHED WITH BEAUTIFUL ENGRAVINGS. / [p.rule] / [p.s.rule] / GLASGOW: / SOLD WHOLESALE BY J. LUMSDEN AND SON. / (TWO-PENCE.)

The TP is on the verso of the front wrapper.

A single gathering of 24 leaves, first and last paste-downs; the second signed E, the eighth F. Pp. 47. Eight leaves of etchings in sanguine, two scenes to each leaf. These leaves are integral in the gathering, unnumbered.

Perhaps *c.* 1815 (the short 's' is used), but a twopenny edition was listed in *Foundations of Learning. c.* 1805 (No. 9).

Wrappers, drab, green, grey-green, salmon pink.

98×61 mm. [Bell; CUL; GlaPL; GlaUL (3 copies); MB; MLG; NLSc; NorBM; Osborne; Rankin; Roscoe; Steedman (Cat. 1978); Stockham; V & A (2 copies); Welch.]

**33. TESTAMENT AND PSALMS.** (*c.* 1805). A Penny Book, listed in No. 9.

**34. DIVINE SONGS.** By Isaac Watts. An edition price 2 *d.* was published in or before 1799, listed in *Elspy Campbell* (No. 64).

**35. DIVINE SONGS.** By Isaac Watts. (*c.* 1805). A Twopenny Book listed in No. 9.

**36. DIVINE SONGS FOR THE USE OF CHILDREN.** By Isaac Watts. n.d. (see note below). Price 6 *d.*

Plate

WATTS / DIVINE SONGS / FOR THE USE OF / CHILDREN / [d.p.rule] / EMBELLISHED WITH FOURTEEN ELEGANT / EMBLEMATICAL DESIGNS. / [engraved t.p. vignette of three heads] / GLASGOW / PUBLISHED BY LUMSDEN & SON / PRICE SIXPENCE. / [scroll] / [p.s.rule].

A single gathering of 26 leaves, signed A at p. [5], A3 at p. 11, B at p. 13, B3 at p. 19, C at p. 21, C3 at p. 27. Pp. 52. The engraved leaves are reckoned in the pagination, but unnumbered. Engraved FP and TP and 6 engraved leaves with 2 engravings to each.

Manuscript date July 10th, 1807 inside Roscoe front wrapper. NLSc copy has paper watermarked '1802'.

Marbled paper wrappers, engraved label on upper cover LUMSDEN & SONS / CHILDRENS LIBRARY / [p.s.rule] /

WATTS, / DIVINE SONGS. / [p.s.rule] / [the whole within a floral wreath.]
126×75 mm. [MB; NLSc; Roscoe; UCLA.]

**37. DIVINE SONGS IN EASY LANGUAGE.** By Isaac Watts. n.d. Price 2*d.*
DIVINE SONGS, / IN EASY LANGUAGE, / FOR THE USE OF / CHILDREN. / [d.p.rule] / BY I. WATTS, D.D. / [d.p.rule] / MATT. XXI. 16. / OUT OF THE MOUTHS OF BABES AND / SUCKLINGS THOU HAST PERFECTED PRAISE. / [d.p.rule] / EDINBURGH: / PRINTED AND SOLD BY G. ROSS. / [p.rule] / PRICE TWO-PENCE.
In a GlaUL copy there are two title-pages, the one reading PUBLISHED BY LUMSDEN & SON, the other PRINTED AND SOLD BY G. ROSS. Probably the extra title-page was tipped in when Lumsden took over from Ross, but the copy is too tightly bound for this to be seen.
Blue wrappers; on the upper the price and the usual FROM /

ROSS'S / JUVENILE / LIBRARY / GLASGOW: / PUBLISHED BY / J. LUMSDEN & SON. Reversible head on lower wrapper. 101×64 mm. [GlaUL.]

ISAAC WATTS, D. D.

DIVINE SONGS,

*IN EASY LANGUAGE,*

FOR THE USE OF

*CHILDREN.*

By I. WATTS, D. D.

*Matt.* xxi. 16.

Out of the mouths of Babes and Sucklings thou haft perfected Praife.

GLASGOW:
Published by
J. LUMSDEN & SON.

1814.

**38. DIVINE SONGS, IN EASY LANGUAGE.** By Isaac Watts. 1814. Price 2*d.* Hugo 320.
Plate
DIVINE SONGS, / IN EASY LANGUAGE, / FOR THE USE OF / CHILDREN / [d.p.rule] / BY I. WATTS, D.D. / [d.p.rule] / MATT. XXI. 16. / OUT OF THE MOUTHS OF BABES AND / SUCKLINGS THOU HAST PERFECTED PRAISE. / [d.p.rule] GLASGOW: / PUBLISHED BY / J. LUMSDEN & SON. / [p.rule] 1814.
A single gathering of 16 leaves, unsigned. Pp. 30[31]. First and last leaves paste-downs. Woodcut FP portrait of Watts and 8 woodcuts in text.
Wrappers: blue-grey, blue, green, yellow, pink boards. Roscoe copy: blue paper wrappers. Text on upper wrapper PRICE

TWOPENCE. / FROM / ROSS'S / JUVENILE / LIBRARY. /
GLASGOW: / PUBLISHED BY / J. LUMSDEN & SON. [Within
a decorative floral frame.] Reversible head on lower wrapper (in
an oval frame).
103×61 mm. [Bell; BM; Bodley; CUL; GlaPL; GlaUL; McEdin;
MLG; NorBM; Rankin; Roscoe (2 copies); UCLA; Welch.]

**39. DIVINE SONGS, IN EASY LANGUAGE.** By Isaac Watts.
n.d. (*c.* 1815). Price 2*d.*
Plate
WATTS' / DIVINE SONGS, / IN / EASY LANGUAGE, / FOR
THE USE OF / CHILDREN. / [oval woodcut of the preacher] /
GLASGOW: / PUBLISHED BY LUMSDEN & SON. / [p.rule] /
PRICE TWOPENCE.
16 leaves of letterpress, 2nd and 3rd signed A2, A3. First and last
paste-downs. Pp. 47. The engraved leaves are reckoned in the
pagination, but are not numbered. 8 leaves of engravings, all

printed in sanguine, and all, except the first having 2 engravings to the page. The FP is on the recto of the first free end paper and faces the TP, which is on the verso of the first paste-down leaf. Drab or purple wrappers.

103×65 mm. [BM; CUL; GlaUL; MB; V & A.]

**40.  DIVINE SONGS, IN EASY LANGUAGE.** By Isaac Watts. Edinburgh, G. Ross. n.d. (? 1815). Price 2 *d.*

DIVINE SONGS, / IN EASY LANGUAGE, / FOR THE USE OF / CHILDREN. / [d.p.rule] / BY I. WATTS, D.D. / [d.p.rule] / MATT. XXI. 16. / OUT OF THE MOUTHS OF BABES AND / SUCKLINGS THOU HAST PERFECTED PRAISE. / [d.p.rule] / EDINBURGH: / PRINTED AND SOLD BY G. ROSS. / [p.rule] / PRICE TWOPENCE.

Format and contents as for No. 38. The blue upper wrapper has the usual 'From Ross's Juvenile Library' within a frame of sapling trees and the usual Lumsden imprint. The lower wrapper has a woodcut of a muffin-man with tray and bell. It seems fairly certain that the Ross edition preceded the Lumsden, and was taken over by Lumsden in or before 1814. This is probably No. B92 (at p. 304) in J. H. P. Pafford's *Isaac Watts' Divine Songs* (O.U.P., 1971) which he dates ? 1815.

103×61 mm. [GlaUL.]

**41.  JESUS CHRIST, LIFE OF.** Edwin Pearson Sale Catalogue, 1868, in lot 195. Perhaps No. 28 or 29.

**42.  JOSEPH AND HIS BRETHREN, THE HISTORY OF.** n.d. (*c.* 1815-20). Price 6 *d.*

THE / HISTORY / OF / JOSEPH / AND / HIS BRETHREN. / [double swelled rule] / [vignette] / GLASGOW. / PUBLISHED BY J. LUMSDEN & SON AT THEIR / TOY BOOK MANU-FACTORY. / PRICE SIXPENCE. / [p.s.rule].

A single gathering of 18 leaves of text, signed in 6's, plus engraved FP and TP and 6 engraved leaves in the text. Pp. 52, the engraved leaves being reckoned in the pagination, but not in the signatures.

Salmon Pink paper wrappers. Engraved label printed on white laid paper. Lettered LUMSDEN & SONS. / CHILDREN'S LIBRARY / [p.rule] / JOSEPH AND HIS / BRETHREN. [Within a double ruled frame.]

115×73 mm. [BM; NLSc.]

# 5

# NURSERY TALES, STORIES & POEMS

*In this list 5 all books are in alphabetical order of the titles omitting 'The', 'An' and the like; and in many cases an adjective preceding the first noun or name of person or place is also omitted, e.g. The Surprising Adventures of Captain Gulliver is listed under 'Adventures'; 'History', 'Renowned History' and such like are also as a rule omitted, e.g. The History of Elspy Campbell is listed under 'Elspy Campbell'. For the authors, see the list at p. 130.*

The Troops of Lilliput marching between the legs of Gulliver.

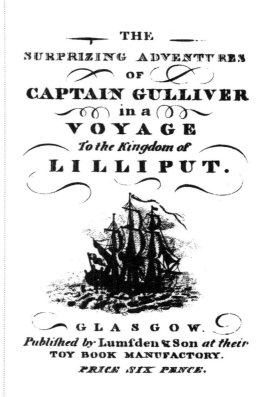

THE SURPRIZING ADVENTURES OF CAPTAIN GULLIVER in a VOYAGE To the Kingdom of LILLIPUT.

GLASGOW.
Published by Lumfden & Son at their
TOY BOOK MANUFACTORY.
PRICE SIX PENCE.

*reduced*

**43. ADVENTURES OF CAPTAIN GULLIVER, THE SURPRISING.** n.d. (not after 1803, see note below). Price 6*d.*
Plate
THE / SURPRISING ADVENTURES / OF / CAPTAIN GULLIVER / IN A / VOYAGE / TO THE KINGDOM OF / LILLIPUT. / [vignette, a three-masted ship] / GLASGOW. / PUBLISHED BY LUMSDEN & SON AT THEIR / TOY BOOK MANUFACTORY. / PRICE SIX PENCE.
A single gathering of 18 leaves plus 8 insets. Pp. 52, the insets being reckoned in the pagination. Engraved FP (Gulliver and the Lilliputian Troops), TP and 6 other engraved leaves.
The BM copy has a mss. inscription inside the front cover 'Miss E. Fleet March 26 1803'.

Pink stiff wrappers, white label on upper: LUMSDEN & SONS. / CHILDRENS LIBRARY. / [d.p.rule] / GULLIVERS TRAVELS [The whole within an ornamental frame of drapery etc.]. 122×78 mm. [BM.]

THE

ADVENTURES

OF

*CAPTAIN GULLIVER,*

IN A VOYAGE TO

LILLIPUT.

GLASGOW:
Published by
J. LUMSDEN & SON.
...........
1814.

**44. ADVENTURES OF CAPTAIN GULLIVER, THE.** 1814. Price 2*d*. Gum. 1558.
Plate
THE / ADVENTURES / OF / CAPTAIN GULLIVER, / IN A VOYAGE TO / LILLIPUT. / [d.p.rule] / GLASGOW: / PUBLISHED BY / J. LUMSDEN & SON. / [rule of dots] / 1814.
In 8's [A-C⁸]. 24 leaves, first and last paste-downs. Pp. 46. Woodcut FP and 12 very crude woodcuts in text.
Drab wrappers; on upper PRICE TWOPENCE. / FROM / ROSS'S / JUVENILE / LIBRARY. / [the Lumsden imprint]. On lower a reversible head, or a woodcut.
99×58 mm. [BM; CUL; MB; NLSc; Ries; UCLA.]

THE

ADVENTURES

OF

CAPTAIN GULLIVER,

IN A VOYAGE TO

LILLIPUT.

GLASGOW,

Publifhed by J Lumsden & Son.

1815.

**45. ADVENTURES OF CAPTAIN GULLIVER, THE.** 1815.
Price 2*d.* Hugo 326.
Plate
THE / ADVENTURES / OF / CAPTAIN GULLIVER, / IN A
VOYAGE TO / LILLIPUT. / [woodcut vignette, a dish of fruit] /
GLASGOW, / PUBLISHED BY J. LUMSDEN & SON. / 1815.
In 8's [A-C⁸]. 24 leaves, first and last paste-downs. Pp. 47.
Woodcut FP and 12 woodcuts in text, repeated from No. 44 but
the type re-set.
Wrappers, grey-green, drab, yellow, purple, blue-grey, grey. On
upper wrapper PRICE TWOPENCE. / FROM / ROSS'S /
JUVENILE / LIBRARY. / [Lumsden's imprint]. On lower a
reversible head.
102×60 mm. [BM; BCE; CUL; ClaPL; GlaUL (4 copies); MLG;
Osborne; Rankin; Roscoe (2 copies); Steedman (Cat. 1978);
UCLA; V & A; Welch.]

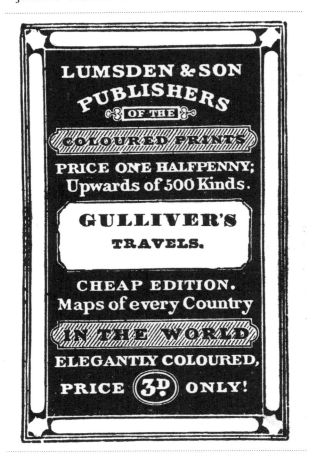

**46. ADVENTURES OF CAPTAIN GULLIVER, THE.** n.d. (a late production, 1830-40). Price 2*d.*
Plate (back cover)
THE / ADVENTURES / OF / CAPTAIN GULLIVER, / IN A / VOYAGE TO LILLIPUT. / [p.rule] / EMBELLISHED WITH / BEAUTIFUL COLOURED PLATES. / [p.rule] / GLASGOW: / PUBLISHED BY J. LUMSDEN & SON.
14 unsigned leaves, first and last paste-downs plus 10 coloured leaves of engravings, 2 to the page.
Green paper wrappers, on the upper LUMSDEN & SON'S / IMPROVED EDITION / OF / COLOURED TWOPENNY BOOKS / EMBELLISHED WITH / NUMEROUS ENGRAV-INGS. . . .
120×79 mm. [GlaUL.]

**ADVENTURES OF FINETTA.** See No. 61.

**47. ALADDIN, THE HISTORY OF.** n.d. Price 2*d.* N.B.L. 418.
THE / HISTORY / OF / ALADDIN; / OR, / THE WONDER-
FUL LAMP. / AN EASTERN TALE. / [p.rule] / EMBEL-
LISHED WITH / BEAUTIFUL COLOURED PLATES. /
[p.rule] / GLASGOW: / PUBLISHED BY J. LUMSDEN & SON.
14 unsigned leaves, inclusive of the wrappers, Pp. 26. Coloured
engraved FP on verso of front wrapper and 10 other coloured
engravings on five leaves, 2 to the page.
Green, grey-green wrappers with design printed in black as for
other titles in this series. Text LUMSDEN & SON'S / IM-
PROVED EDITION / OF / COLOURED / TWOPENNY
BOOKS / EMBELLISHED WITH / NUMEROUS ENGRAV-
INGS / ALADDIN, / OR / THE WONDERFUL LAMP. [within
a frame] / [emblem with 'Let Glasgow Flourish'] / LUMSDEN &
SON / 20 QUEEN STREET. Back cover advertises Coloured
Prints and Maps, with title in centre panel.
121×78 mm. [GlaUL; Moon.]

**ALI BABA AND MORGIANA.** See *The Story of the Forty Thieves*
(No. 125).

**48. AMUSING RIDDLE BOOK, THE.** (*c.* 1820). A Halfpenny
Book, listed in No. 8. *The title is fairly common. See Lauriston, pp.
194-95.*

**49. AMUSING RIDDLE BOOK, THE.** (*c.* 1815-20). Another
edition. 2*d.* plain, 3*d.* coloured. Advertised in No. 92. No copy
located.

**50. BABES IN THE WOOD, THE.** (*c.* 1805). A Penny Book,
listed in No. 9.
*Darton goes badly wrong in saying Sarah Trimmer, born in 1741 at
Ipswich, read and enjoyed when she was young,* The Babes in the
Wood, *in a chapbook edition published by Lumsden of Glasgow. Unless
there was an earlier Lumsden, she must have read the chapbook when she
was about 60 years of age. It may be that Mrs Trimmer's memory was at
fault in referring to a Glasgow printer. There was a printer Thomas
Lumsden operating in Edinburgh in 1727-49.*

**51. BABES IN THE WOOD, THE.** (*c.* 1820). A Halfpenny
Book, listed in No. 8.

**52. BABES IN THE WOOD, THE.** (*c.* 1815-20). Another edition. 2*d.* plain, 3*d.* coloured. Listed in No. 92. No copy located.

FRONTISPIECE

The Beast

ATTACKING the MERCHANT

*reduced*

BEAUTY

AND

*THE BEAST.*

*A TALE.*

FOR THE ENTERTAINMENT OF

*Juvenile Readers.*

*Ornamented with Elegant Engravings.*

Glasgow:

Published and Sold by J. LUMSDEN & SON.

*Price Sixpence.*

**53. BEAUTY AND THE BEAST.** n.d (see note below). Price 6*d.* Hugo 4270.
Plate
BEAUTY / AND / THE BEAST. / A TALE. / FOR THE ENTERTAINMENT OF / JUVENILE READERS. / [d.p.rule] / ORNAMENTED WITH ELEGANT ENGRAVINGS. / [d.p.rule] / [d.p.rule] / GLASGOW: / PUBLISHED AND SOLD BY J. LUMSDEN & SON. / [p.rule] / PRICE SIXPENCE.
A single gathering of 24 leaves, signed A2 at p. 13, A3, at p. 17, A4 at p. 23. Engraved FP and 5 other engraved leaves. Pp. 48

[49]. The engraved leaves are reckoned in the pagination, but are not numbered. The last engraved leaf is conjugate with the FP leaf and consequently follows the last leaf of text. Small oval woodcut at p. 48, which Hugo records as 'thought to be by Thomas Bewick'. It might perhaps have been done in his workshop.

Stiff paper wrappers with engraved label on upper cover lettered LUMSDEN & SON'S / EDITION / OF BEAUTY AND / THE BEAST. / [Within a decorative border.]

To be dated not before 1818. There are watermarks of that year and 1817.

130×88 mm. [BCE; BM; Elkin Mathews (Cat. 163); GlaUL; Maxwell Hunley (Cat. 48); MLG; NLSc; Osborne; Roscoe (2 copies).]

**54. BLUE BEARD, THE HISTORY OF.** n.d. (*c.* 1830). Price 1*d.*

TP on recto of front wrapper: [p. rule] / NO. XVIII. / [p.rule] / THE / HISTORY / OF / BLUE BEARD. / [p.rule] / PRICE ONE PENNY. / [p.rule] / GLASGOW: / PUBLISHED BY / JAMES LUMSDEN & SON. [The whole within a decorative frame with large bowl of flowers at top.]

Lower wrapper: THE / HISTORY / OF / BLUE BEARD. / [p.rule] / GLASGOW: / PUBLISHED BY J. LUMSDEN & SON / 20, QUEEN-STREET. [The whole enclosed within the shaped design of a flying balloon with decorative scrolls at bottom. Inside this scroll are the words ONE PENNY.]

10 pp. the first and last of which are pasted to the inside of the covers. 6 wood-engravings. No separate title-page.

*Apparently a different version of the story of this name in* Tales of Mother Goose *(No. 66).*

(Communicated.)

137×82 mm. [NLSc.]

**55. BLUE BEARD, THE HISTORY OF.** (*c.* 1815-20). Another edition. 2*d.* plain, 3*d.* coloured. Listed in No. 92. No copy located.

**BLUE BEARD.** See also *Entertaining Tales of Mother Goose* (No. 66).

**CHILDREN IN THE WOOD.** See *The History of John Gilpin* (Nos. 89, 89a).

**56. CHRISTMAS TALES FOR THE AMUSEMENT AND INSTRUCTION OF YOUNG LADIES AND GENTLEMEN.** n.d. (*c.* 1804). Price 6*d.*

CHRISTMAS TALES / FOR THE / AMUSEMENT AND INSTRUCTION / OF / YOUNG LADIES AND GENTLEMEN / IN / WINTER EVENINGS. / [d.p.rule] / EMBELLISHED WITH EIGHT ELEGANT ENGRAVINGS. / [engraved vignette] / GLASGOW, / PUBLISHED BY LUMSDEN & SON / PRICE SIXPENCE.

Irregular format. 18 leaves of letterpress plus 8 engraved leaves, the latter reckoned in the pagination, but unnumbered; 2 engravings to each leaf. Pp. 52.

118×70 mm. [Sotheby, 16 March 1970, lot 218 (no wrappers).]

**57. CHRISTMAS TALES FOR THE INSTRUCTION OF GOOD BOYS AND GIRLS.** By Mr. Solomon Sobersides. n.d. (see note below). Price 6*d.* Hugo 4267.

CHRISTMAS / TALES / FOR THE INSTRUCTION / OF / GOOD BOYS AND GIRLS, / BY / MR. SOLOMON SOBER-SIDES. / [p.s.rule] / EMBELLISHED WITH ENGRAVINGS / [oval vignette] / GLASGOW. / PUBLISHED BY LUMSDEN & SON. / & SOLD BY STODDART & CRAGGS, HULL / PRICE SIXPENCE.

A single gathering of 24 leaves of text plus engraved FP and TP and 6 other engraved leaves. The first, second, fifth, sixth and tenth leaves of text are signed A, A2, B, B2, C2. The engraved leaves, other than the FP, are reckoned in the pagination, but are unnumbered. Pp. 61[62]. Small oval woodcut at p. 61. Advertisement by Lumsden on p. [62].

Can be dated 1814 or later: watermark 1814 in leaf A1.

Stiff glossy paper wrappers, blue, pale green. Engraved label on front wrapper LUMSDEN & SONS, / CHILDREN'S LIBRARY, / [p.s.rule] / CHRISTMAS / TALES. [Within a frame of ornate cornucopias.]

*Though written in full awareness of the Trimmer school of teaching, and amply ornamented with morality and pious example, the eleven stories in this book are not insufferable. The final story, 'The Three Wishes' actually introduces a fairy and records the remarkable doings of a black pudding; not at all in the Trimmer tradition.*

111×82 mm. [Bell; Elkin Mathews (Cat. 163); MB; NLSc; OUP; Roscoe; V & A.]

**58. CINDERELLA, OR THE LITTLE GLASS SLIPPER.** (*c.* 1815-20). 2*d.* plain, 3*d.* coloured. Advertised in No. 92. No copy located.

**CINDERELLA.** See also *Entertaining Tales of Mother Goose* (No. 66).

**COCK ROBIN.** See Nos. 60, 62, 63.

**59. COTTAGE TALES FOR LITTLE PEOPLE.** n.d. (1815-20). Price 2*d.* Hugo 319.
COTTAGE TALES / FOR / LITTLE PEOPLE; / OR, THE / AMUSING REPOSITORY, / FOR ALL / GOOD BOYS AND GIRLS. / [woodcut in a rectangular frame, cottages and a distant church steeple] / GLASGOW: / PUBLISHED AND SOLD WHOLESALE, / BY LUMSDEN & SON, / [PRICE TWOPENCE.]
A single gathering of 16 unsigned leaves. Pp. 32. 9 woodcuts, those at pp. 3, 6, 11, 15, 20 ape John Bewick, but are hardly good enough for Lee.
Wrappers, blue, pink, salmon pink, yellow, some without text or woodcuts, others show agricultural or rural scenes, with text. Variant texts and woodcuts on the wrappers are numerous. Some are copies after Bewick.
102×62 mm. [Bell; BM; Bodley; GlaPL; GlaUL (5 copies); Maxwell Hunley (Cat. 48); MLG; Rankin; Renier; Roscoe (2 copies); Steedman (Cat. 1978); V & A (3 copies); Welch; Wood.]

**60. DEATH AND BURIAL OF COCK ROBIN, THE HISTORY OF THE.** n.d.
A single sheet for decorating the nursery, printed on one side only. 8 hand-coloured engravings each measuring *c.* 43×50 mm. Four lines of verse below each cut. Peter Opie suggests these cuts were also used in an edition of the poem in book form.
There is no direct evidence as to dating but the period 1815-35 is suggested.
140×224 mm. [Opie.]

**61. DISCREET PRINCESS, THE.** 1818. Hugo 413.
Plate
THE / DISCREET PRINCESS; / OR, / THE ADVENTURES OF / FINETTA. / AN / ENTERTAINING STORY / FOR THE AMUSEMENT OF / YOUNG MASTERS AND MISSES. / [d.p.rule] / GLASGOW: / PUBLISHED BY J. LUMSDEN & SON. / [wavy rule] / 1818.
Two gatherings of 18 and 12 leaves. Signatures: 5th leaf A2, 7th leaf A3, 19th leaf B, 21st leaf B2, 23rd leaf B3, 24th leaf B4. Last leaf a blank. Pp. viii,[9]-57. Woodcut FP and 12 whole page woodcuts in text.

FRONTISPIECE.

*See pages* 20, 21.

THE

# DISCREET PRINCESS:

OR,

THE ADVENTURES OF

# FINETTA.

AN

ENTERTAINING STORY

For the Amusement of

*YOUNG MASTERS AND MISSES.*

GLASGOW:

PUBLISHED BY J. LUMSDEN & SON.

1818.

*reduced*

Stiff paper wrappers, blue-grey, yellow, pink; engraved yellow label on front wrapper LUMSDEN & SONS / EDITION / OF / FINETTA. (in a frame).
*Translated by Robert Samber (translator of the Perrault 'Mother Goose Tales') from* L'Adroite Princesse *of Marie Jeanne L'Heritier de Villardon. The letter of dedication of this edition to Lady Mary Montague is signed by Samber.*
   *Hugo speaks of the woodcuts as being 'apparently by John Bewick'. This is doubtful; they might be by Lee.*
133×88 mm. [BM (dated 1878 in the catalogue); CUL; GlaUL; MB: NLSc; Roscoe; Schiller (Cat. 29); Traylen; V & A (2 copies); Welch.]

AN ELEGY

ON THE

## DEATH AND BURIAL

OF

### COCK-ROBIN.

Little Robin Red-breast,
Sat upon a pole;
Wiggle waggle went his tail,
Which made him look quite droll.

GLASGOW:
*Published and Sold, Wholesale,*
BY LUMSDEN AND SON,
[Price One Penny.]

WHO kill'd Cock Robin?

I, says the Sparrow,

With my bow and arrow,

And I kill'd Cock Robin.

This is the Sparrow,

With his bow and arrow.

**62. ELEGY ON THE DEATH AND BURIAL OF COCK ROBIN, AN.** n.d. (*c.* 1815-20). Price 1*d.* Hugo 4271 (but specifies 'Pp. 14').
Plate
AN ELEGY / ON THE / DEATH AND BURIAL / OF / COCK-ROBIN. / [woodcut of a bird in an oval frame] / LITTLE ROBIN REDBREAST, / SAT UPON A POLE; / WIGGLE WAGGLE WENT HIS TAIL, / WHICH MADE HIM LOOK QUITE DROLL. / [p.s.rule] / GLASGOW: / PUBLISHED AND SOLD, WHOLESALE, / BY LUMSDEN AND SON, / [PRICE ONE PENNY.]
A gathering of 8 unsigned leaves. Pp. 13[16]. The TP is on the verso of the first leaf, on the recto a woodcut FP of a donkey in an ornamental frame. 13 small woodcuts, and a whole page woodcut of a bear (in a frame) on verso of the last leaf, very possibly copied after Bewick.
Pink wrappers (BM copy); on the upper a woodcut of a Post Boy and text FROM / LUMSDEN & SONS / JUVENILE LIBRARY,

/ 60, QUEEN-STREET, / GLASGOW. On lower a woodcut 'Leaping a Rivulet'.

*Opie (Nursery Rhymes Pp. 129-33.) has a good deal to say about variant versions of the four lines of verse.*
101×63 mm. [BM.]

**63. ELEGY ON THE DEATH AND BURIAL OF COCK ROBIN, AN.** n.d. (a late printing probably *c.* 1830). Price 1*d.* LUMSDEN AND SON'S SUPERIOR EDITION / OF PENNY BOOKS. / [p.rule] / AN ELEGY / ON THE / DEATH AND BURIAL / OF / COCK ROBIN. / [p.rule] / [woodcut of a robin in a rectangular frame] / [p.rule] / PRICE ONE PENNY. / [p.rule] / GLASGOW: / PUBLISHED BY LUMSDEN & SON.
5 unsigned and unnumbered leaves. 12 oval woodcuts in the text flanked with printers' ornaments. The whole printed on a buff paper. No wrappers on the only copy seen.
130×81 mm. [Renier.]

**64. ELSPY CAMPBELL, THE HISTORY OF.** 1799. Price 1*d.* THE / HISTORY / OF / ELSPY CAMPBELL. / PRESENTED TO ALL GOOD / LITTLE MASTERS AND MISSES, / IN CHRISTENDOM. / [p.rule] / EMBELLISHED WITH COPPERPLATES. / [p.rule] / GLASGOW: / SOLD WHOLE-SALE BY J. LUMSDEN & SON, / AT THEIR TOY-BOOK MANUFACTORY. / 1799. / (PRICE ONE PENNY.)
24 unsigned leaves, inclusive of upper and lower wrappers. Pp. 6-20. The engraved FP of 'Elspy Campbell' is on the recto of the leaf following the title leaf. Whole page engravings at pp. [10], [15] and [24]. All the engravings are printed in sanguine. List of books, 'toy-cards', etc. on the recto of p. [25]. The wrappers are remarkable for their woodcut (? engraved) decorations of 'Rabbit' and 'Mouse'.
*The tale is extracted from the story of 'Old Lawrence' in Lucas Williams' translation of Berquin's Children's Friend.*
102×62 mm. [Osborne (but not listed in Catalogues 1 and 2).]

**ENTERTAINING AND INSTRUCTIVE HISTORY OF LITTLE JACK.** See *Little Jack*. (No. 93).

**65. ENTERTAINING STORY, THE, OF LITTLE CINDERELLA AND THE GLASS SLIPPER, FROM THE TALES OF MOTHER GOOSE.** n.d. Price 1*d.* Welch, 896. 1. (p. 71). GLASGOW: PUBLISHED AND SOLD WHOLESALE BY LUMSDEN AND SON.
[Ball.]

FRONTISPIECE.

Here Mother Goose in winter nights
The old and young she both delights:

(The)

ENTERTAINING TALES

OF

(Mother Goose)

for

THE AMUSEMENT OF YOUTH,

Embelished with Elegant Engravings.

GLASGOW
Published by Jas. Lumsden & Son
Price Sixpence

*reduced*

## 66. ENTERTAINING TALES OF MOTHER GOOSE, THE.

n.d. (not before 1817, see note below). By Charles Perrault. Price
6*d*. Welch, 894.1. (p. 62).
Plate
THE / ENTERTAINING TALES / OF / MOTHER GOOSE /
FOR / THE AMUSEMENT OF YOUTH, / [p.rule] / EM-
BELISHED WITH ELEGANT ENGRAVINGS. / [p.rule]
[vignette] / GLASGOW / PUBLISHED BY JAS. LUMSDEN &
SON. / PRICE SIXPENCE.
A single gathering of 18 leaves of text plus engraved FP and TP
and 6 other engraved leaves. Pp. 36; the engraved leaves not
reckoned in the pagination. The first leaf of text is signed A, the
fifth A2, the seventh A3, and the ninth A4.

The tales are *Little Red Riding-Hood, Blue Beard, The Fairy, Cinderilla* and *Riquet with the Tuft.*

A copy in the Roscoe collection has the watermark date 1817. Buff stiff paper wrappers, deep yellow, rose, drab. Engraved pink rectangular label on front wrapper LUMSDEN & SON'S / NEW EDITION OF / MOTHER GOOSE [in an ornamental frame].

137×86 mm. [BM; Boston P.L.; Brimmell; MLG; NLSc; Roscoe (2 copies); V & A; Wood.]

**FAIRY, THE.** See No. 66.

**67. FAIRY TALES OF MOTHER GOOSE,** 1814. Presumably based on Perrault. (Reported by UCLA.) Possibly No. 70. [MB; McKell.]

**68. FAIRY TALES OF MOTHER GOOSE: CONTAINING THE STORIES OF CINDERELLA.** n.d. (The 'Mother Goose' presumably based on Perrault.) Price 2*d.* Welch, 894.1. (p. 62). [Ball.]

Old Mother Goose, in Winter nights,
Good Boys and Girls she here delights.

FAIRY TALES

OF

PAST TIMES,

FROM

*MOTHER GOOSE.*

EDINBURGH:

Printed and Sold by G. Ross,
Horse Wynd.

1805.

[*Price Two Pence.*]

**69. FAIRY TALES OF PAST TIMES, FROM MOTHER GOOSE.** (By Charles Perrault). 1805. Price 2*d*.
Plate
The name of G. Ross of Edinburgh is on the TP, that of J. Lumsden & Son on the front wrapper.
FAIRY TALES / OF / PAST TIMES, / FROM / MOTHER GOOSE. / [woodcut vignette, a dish of fruit] / EDINBURGH: / PRINTED AND SOLD BY G. ROSS, / HORSE WYND. / [d.p.rule] / 1805. / [PRICE TWO PENCE.]
In 8's [A-C⁸]. 24 leaves, first and last paste-downs. Pp. 47.
Woodcut FP 'Mother Goose' and 8 woodcut head and tail-pieces in the text.
Drab or yellow wrappers. On the upper PRICE TWOPENCE. / FROM / ROSS'S / JUVENILE / LIBRARY. (in an ornamental surround of leaves) / GLASGOW: / PUBLISHED BY / J. LUMSDEN & SON. The V & A copy has a reversible head on the lower wrapper.
98×60 mm. [Bell; V & A.]

**70. FAIRY TALES OF PAST TIMES, FROM MOTHER GOOSE.** (By Charles Perrault.) 1814. Price 2*d*. Hugo 322.
FP as for Ross's 1805 edition (No. 69); so also with the TP, except for the imprint which reads GLASGOW: / PUBLISHED BY / J. LUMSDEN & SON. / [p.rule] / 1814.
In 8's [A-C⁸]. Contents, etc. as for the 1805 edition, of which the present copy will probably be found to be a re-issue of the original sheets with a revised TP.
Drab wrappers, FROM / ROSS'S / JUVENILE / LIBRARY and Lumsden's imprint on the front, a reversible head or other woodcut on the lower.
99×60 mm. [Bodley; MB; NLSc; NorBM; V & A.]

**FAMILY AT SMILEDALE, HISTORY OF THE.** See No. 136.

**FINETTA.** See No. 61.

**FORTY THIEVES, THE.** See No. 125.

**71. FRIENDS, THE.** 1810. Price 4*d*. 'Friend's' is the spelling in the TP; in the running title it is 'Friends'.
Plate
THE / FRIEND'S; / OR THE / HISTORY / OF / BILLY FREEMAN / AND / TOMMY TRUELOVE. / PROPER TO BE IMITATED BY ALL THOSE / WHO DESIRE TO BE / GOOD AND GREAT / [d.p.rule] / GLASGOW, / PRINTED FOR J

THE

# F R I E N D'S;

OR THE

## HISTORY

OF

## BILLY FREEMAN

AND

## TOMMY TRUELOVE.

Proper to be *imitated* by all those
Who desire to be
### GOOD AND GREAT.

GLASGOW,

Printed for J Lumsden & Son
[*Price Four Pence.*]
1810.

*Cuts by Bewick.*

LUMSDEN & SON. / [PRICE FOUR PENCE.] / 1810.
In 8's [A-F⁸]. 48 leaves. Pp 96. 20 crude woodcuts. Pp. 82-96
comprise *The History of Miss Nancy Truelove.*
*There was an edition by John Marshall in 179–, shown in the Malvern
Exhibition, 1911, Item 167.*
97×55 mm. [Osborne, but not listed in the printed catalogues.
Rebound.]

**72. FUN UPON FUN; OR THE HUMOURS OF A FAIR.** n.d.
(see note below). Price 2*d.* Hugo 318.
Plate
FUN UPON FUN; / OR THE / HUMOURS OF A FAIR. /
GIVING A DESCRIPTION OF THE CURIOUS / AMUSE-
MENTS IN EARLY LIFE: / ALSO AN ACCOUNT OF A /
MOUNTEBANK DOCTOR / AND HIS / MERRY ANDREW. /
[oval woodcut of a boy running] / GLASGOW: / SOLD
WHOLESALE BY J. LUMSDEN AND SON. / [PRICE
TWOPENCE.]
In 8's [A-B⁸]. 16 leaves of text plus 8 engraved leaves. Pp. 47, the

*FUN UPON FUN;*

OR THE

## HUMOURS OF A FAIR.

Giving a Description of the Curious

*AMUSEMENTS IN EARLY LIFE:*

ALSO AN ACCOUNT OF A

MOUNTEBANK DOCTOR

AND HIS

*MERRY ANDREW.*

GLASGOW:

Sold wholesale by J. Lumsden and Son.

[*Price Twopence.*]

first and last leaves paste-downs. The TP is on the paste-down inside the front wrapper. The FP is a free leaf (recto blank). Lettered MERRY ANDREW / [woodcut of youth flourishing a brush while dancing.] / In ev'ry rank you'll Merry Andrews find, / Who with their nonsense oft decieve Mankind. Lettered in a half circle within a decorative surround. The engraved leaves, printed in sanguine, bistre or sepia, are reckoned in the pagination, but are unnumbered. The oval woodcut on the TP varies: in some copies it shows a horse in harness. The 3 small woodcuts were claimed by Hugo to be by Bewick. All that can be said for them is that they show his influence; they might conceivably have come from his workshop.

Copies examined have watermark dates 1816 and 182[ ], the latter possibly to be read as 1820.

Wrappers, brown, orange-pink, pink, grey-green, pale grey-green, buff, drab, green. No text on wrappers.

*A very mixed bag: Sam Gooseberry's Account of the wonderful Things of the Fair, The Doctor's Speech, Sam Sensible's Account of what he had seen in the Fair, Descant on Time, On Learning, Business, Idleness, etc.*

*One of the most popular of the Lumsden juveniles. Fun upon Fun was also the title for one of the Lumsden Chapbooks proper (see No. 152). In this form it also seems to have been something of a best seller. Lauriston lists some 18 editions by various publishers.*
100×62 mm. [Aberdeen; BCE; BM; Bodley; Bell; Brimmell; CUL (2 copies); Elkin Mathews (Cat. 163); GlaPL; GlaUL (3 copies); Hornel; Hyde-Parker; MB; NorBM; Osborne; Rankin; Ries; Roscoe (2 copies); Steedman (Cat. 1978); V & A; Wellcome.]

**73. GENTLE SHEPHERD, THE.** By Alan Ramsay. n. d. (*c.* 1815-20).
THE / *GENTLE SHEPHERD,* / A / SCOTS PASTORAL / COMEDY. / [d.p.rule] / BY / ALLAN RAMSAY. / [d.p.rule] / [swelled rule] / GLASGOW: / PUBLISHED BY J. LUMSDEN & SON.
Pp. [i-iii], iv-v, [vi], vii-xi, [12-13], 14-89. Verso of 89 blank. Engraved frontispiece. Imprint of J. Neilson, printer on p. 89. Covers printed in black on grey paper, and pasted over endpapers. Lettered GENTLE / [woodcut] / SHEPHERD. [d.p.rule above and below] [The whole within a decorative frame.] Back cover has 4 woodcuts within decorative frame. (Communicated.)
134×83 mm. [NLSc.]

**74. GILES GINGERBREAD, THE HISTORY OF.** (*c.* 1820). A Halfpenny Book, listed in No. 8.

**75. GILES GINGERBREAD, THE HISTORY OF.** (*c.* 1805). A Penny Book, listed in No. 9.

**76. GILES GINGERBREAD, THE HISTORY OF.** n.d. (*c.* 1830-40). Price 1 *d.*
TP on recto of front wrapper: LUMSDEN & SON'S SUPERIOR EDITION OF PENNY BOOKS. / [p.rule] / THE / HISTORY / OF / GILES GINGERBREAD. / [a woodcut] / [p. rule] / GLASGOW: / PUBLISHED BY LUMSDEN & SON. [The whole within a rectangular ornamental frame.]
6 unsigned leaves, inclusive of the wrappers. Pp. 11. 7 small woodcuts in text, flanked by printer's ornaments.
Lower wrapper GILES / GINGERBREAD. / [woodcut] /

GLASGOW: / PUBLISHED BY LUMSDEN & SON. Pink wrappers.

*For earlier use of the title see Nos. 74 and 75, and NBL, p. 107 and Roscoe, Newbery, J267. Has been attributed to John Newbery, Goldsmith, Griffith Jones, Giles Jones. An edition published by J. Kendrew of York, c. 1820 (copy in Osborne, p. 314), gives 'Tom Trip' as the author.*

130×77 mm. [BM.]

**77. GILES GINGERBREAD, THE HISTORY OF.** (*c.* 1815-20). Another edition. 2 *d.* plain, 3 *d.* coloured. Listed in No. 92. No copy located.

**GOODY TWO SHOES, HISTORY OF.** *One of the most popular books of this period for children. Welch (Vol. D-G, Nos 427.1) takes nearly 4 pp. to list (with the minimum of detail) the English and American editions up to about 1830. There were later editions as well, reprints and piracies. See Spielmann & Layard, 1905, pp. 285-89. The Sotheby Catalogue of Juvenilia, Part III, for 16th October, 1975, lists 34 editions of the work by various publishers, from the 2nd edition, 1766 (lot 1197) to c. 1840. There have been later editions as well, and the facsimile of the 3rd edition, 1766, edited by Welsh in 1881.*

**78. GOODY TWO SHOES, THE RENOWNED HISTORY OF.** n.d. (*c.* 1805). Price 6 *d.*
THE / RENOWNED / HISTORY / OF / GOODY TWO SHOES. / [d.p.rule] / EMBELLISHED WITH FOURTEEN ELEGANT / COPPER PLATE PRINTS / [p.s.rule] / [vignette, a church with spire] / GLASGOW, / PUBLISHED BY LUMSDEN & SON AT THEIR / TOY BOOK MANUFACTORY. / [PRICE SIXPENCE]
Engraved TP and FP.
(Communicated.)
[Welch.]

**79. GOODY TWO SHOES, THE HISTORY OF, WITH THE ADVENTURES OF HER BROTHER TOMMY.** n.d. (1818 or after: see note below). Price 6 *d.* ? NBL 641. ? Gum. 2759.
Plate
THE / HISTORY / OF / GOODY TWO SHOES / WITH THE / ADVENTURES / OF HER / BROTHER TOMMY / [p.s.rule] / EMBELLISHED WITH ELEGANT ENGRAVINGS / [vignette] / GLASGOW / PUBLISHED BY J. LUMSDEN & SON. / & SOLD BY STODDART & CRAGGS, HULL. / PRICE SIXPENCE.

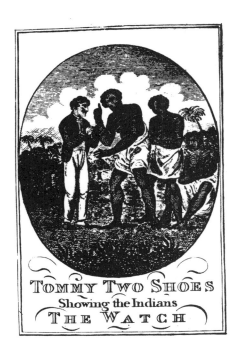

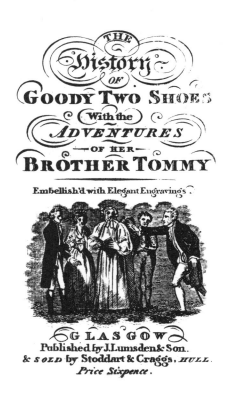

*reduced*

A single gathering of 18 leaves of text, first signed A, third A3, fourth B, sixth B3, seventh C, ninth C3, plus engraved FP and TP and 6 other engraved leaves. Pp. 52, the engraved leaves reckoned in the pagination, but not numbered. Small woodcuts at pp. 51 and 52.

Watermarks 1814 and 1818 seen in copies examined.

Stiff paper wrappers, red, drab, grey-blue, pink, grey-green, grey, blue-grey. White label on upper wrapper HISTORY OF / GOODY TWO SHOES / AND HER BROTHER / TOMMY. 132×84 mm. [BM (3 copies); Bodley; CUL; Elkin Mathews (Cat. 163); GlaUL; MB; MLG; NLSc; Osborne; Roscoe (2 copies); V & A; Welch.]

## 80. GOODY TWO SHOES, THE HISTORY OF.

W. M. Stone, in his article *The History of Little Goody Two-Shoes* in *American Antiquarian Society Proceedings*, N.S. 49, 1939, at pp. 364-5 lists the following. Details as given by Stone.

1810. THE HIST: &c. Glasgow. J. Lumsden & Son. n.d. *c.* 1810. Copy: N.Y. Pub. Lib.

1820. THE HIST: &c. Glasgow. J. Lumsden. FP and 14 cuts. n.d. *c.* 1820.

1825. THE RENOWNED HIST: &c. Glasgow: Lumsden & Son. n.d. *c.* 1825. 14 plates. Copy: Bates.

1830. THE HISTORY: &c. Glasgow: Lumsden. Engravings. n.d. *c.* 1830. Copies: Stone, Ball.

1830. THE HISTORY: &c. Glasgow: Published by J. Lumsden & Son and sold by Stoddard & Craggs, Hull. n.d. *c.* 1830. Copy: Ball. [This presumably is No. 79.]

**FRONTISPIECE.**

*See Page 47.*

THE

**HISTORY**

OF

𝕬𝕽𝕬𝕮𝕴𝕺𝕾𝕬

AND

**PERCINET.**

𝔄 𝔉𝔞𝔦𝔯𝔶 𝔗𝔞𝔩𝔢.

EMBELLISHED WITH ELEGANT CUTS.

GLASGOW:

PUBLISHED BY J. LUMSDEN AND SON.

[*Price Sixpence.*]

*reduced*

**81. GRACIOSA AND PERCINET, THE HISTORY OF.** By Marie Catherine de la Mothe, Comtesse d'Aulnoy. n.d. Price 6 *d.* Plate
THE / HISTORY / OF / GRACIOSA / AND / PERCINET. / A FAIRY TALE. / [p.rule] / EMBELLISHED WITH ELEGANT CUTS / [p.rule] / GLASGOW: / PUBLISHED BY J. LUMSDEN AND SON. / [p.rule] / [PRICE SIXPENCE.]
In 6's [A-D⁶ E²]. 26 leaves. Pp. 51. Woodcut FP and 11 other woodcuts in text.
Date about 1820. Mozley of Gainsborough had done editions of this in or after 1798 and in 1806. (NBL, 421, 422; Hugo 213.) 129×83 mm. [V & A.]

**82. HENRY JOHNSTON, HISTORY OF.** (*c.* 1815-20). 2 *d.* plain, 3 *d.* coloured. Listed in No. 92. No copy located.

**83. HENRY JOHNSTON, HISTORY OF.** (*c.* 1820). A Halfpenny book, listed in No. 128. No copy located.

**83a. HENRY ROBINSON, HISTORY OF.** Recorded by Mr Roscoe as being listed in one of Lumsden's Halfpenny Books, *Familiar Objects Described, c.* 1820 (No. 8.) This may be an error as other lists in Halfpenny Books located give the title as *History of Henry Johnston.* Unfortunately at this time it cannot be checked as the only copy of *Familar Objects Described* located in the Renier collection has gone astray during transfer to the Victoria & Albert Museum.

**84. HOLIDAY ENTERTAINMENT.** n.d. (*c.* 1820). Price 2 *d.* Hugo 317.
HOLIDAY ENTERTAINMENT; / OR, THE / GOOD CHILD'S FAIRING. / CONTAINING THE / PLAYS AND SPORTS / OF / CHARLES AND BILLY WELLDON, / AND OTHER / LITTLE BOYS AND GIRLS WHO WENT / WITH THEM TO THE FAIR. / [woodcut within an oval frame of stately home on rising ground with trees] / GLASGOW: / PUBLISHED AND SOLD WHOLESALE, / BY LUMSDEN AND SON. / [PRICE TWOPENCE.]
16 leaves, the 5th signed B. Pp. 31[32]. 8 woodcuts, those on TP and last page of better quality than the 6 in text, each of which is oval within a rectangular frame. Many of the cuts are spoiled by poor inking.

The wrappers have numerous variations and cover colours, & unusually large woodcuts on both wrappers. With text FROM / LUMSDEN & SON'S / JUVENILE LIBRARY, / [woodcut] / 60, QUEEN-STREET, GLASGOW. / PRICE TWOPENCE.
*One of the commonest of the Lumsden juveniles. The activities of 4 children on holiday. Charley, Billy, Sally and Nancy are recounted. Inevitably the children are either good or naughty, so that the usual morals can be drawn by the chorus of grown-ups.*
BCE.   No wrappers.
Bell.   Yellow wrappers. Woodcut of children 'Riding on two horses' on each cover.
BM, 12804.de.57[2], blue wrappers, woodcut of a lion; another copy 12804.de.65(4), blue wrappers, woodcuts of 'Harrowing' and 'Ploughing'.
Bodley.   No wrappers.
CUL.   Blue wrappers, woodcuts of 'Man on horseback', 'Schoolmaster and bad boy'. Another copy, salmon pink wrappers, 'Riding on two horses' and 'Riding one Horse'.
GlaUL.   4 copies. One has salmon pink wrappers, woodcuts of 'Boys marching' and 'Boy with donkey'.
Osborne.   Pink wrappers.
Roscoe.   3 copies. Blue and yellow wrappers with various cuts.
Shepard.   Pale yellow wrappers. Woodcuts of 'Ships coming out of port' and 'Under sail'.
V & A.   Salmon pink wrappers. Woodcuts of 'Ship' on each wrapper. Another in yellow wrappers with woodcuts 'Harrowing' and 'Ploughing'.
100×65 mm. [Aberdeen (2 copies); BCE; Bell; BM (2 copies); Bodley; CUL (2 copies); GlaPL; GlaUL (4 copies); Hornel; MB; MLG; Osborne; Rankin; Roscoe (3 copies); Rylands; Shepard; Steedman (Cat. 1978); V & A; Welch.]


**85. HOUSE THAT JACK BUILT, THE.** (*c.* 1820). Price ½*d*.
THE / HOUSE / THAT / JACK BUILT. / [wavy line] / [woodcut of the house] / [wavy line] / GLASGOW: / JAMES LUMSDEN AND SON. / [p.rule] / PRICE ONE HALF-PENNY. [Decorative border surround.]
A single gathering of 8 unsigned leaves, including covers. Pp. 16 (numbered 4 to 15). 14 woodcuts including one on the back wrapper with list of other titles in the series listed below. With an alphabet. A book of this title was published by Ross of Edinburgh, price 1*d*.
95×60 mm. [MLG.]

**86. JACK AND THE BEANSTALK.** n.d. (1830-40). Price 2*d.*
THE HISTORY / OF / JACK / AND / THE BEAN-STALK. / [p.rule] / EMBELLISHED WITH / BEAUTIFUL COLOURED PLATES. / [p.rule] / GLASGOW: / PUBLISHED BY J. LUMSDEN & SON. [The whole within a single line border with a cross at each corner.]
Pp. 26. Frontispiece and 10 woodcuts on 5 leaves. All hand-coloured. Frontis. and last plate on verso of covers.
Lumsden's 'Improved edition of coloured Twopenny Books' series.
120×80 mm. [Osborne (not listed in the printed catalogue).]

**87. JACK THE GIANT-KILLER.** n.d. (*c.* 1815-20).
JACK / THE / GIANT-KILLER; / BEING / THE HISTORY / OF ALL / HIS WONDERFUL EXPLOITS AGAINST THE / GIANTS. / [p.rule] / EMBELLISHED WITH / BEAUTIFUL COLOURED PLATES. / [p.rule] / GLASGOW: / PUBLISHED BY J. LUMSDEN & SON.
Pp. [1-4], 5-6, [7-8], 9-12, [13-16], 17-20, [21-22], 23-26, [27-28].
11 hand-coloured wood-engravings, two to a page except for the frontispiece. Woodcut covers uniform with *Mynheer Von Wodenblock.* Printed in black on grey paper and pasted to pp. 1 and 28. Cover title JACK, / THE / GIANT KILLER.
(Communicated.)
120×80 mm. [NLSc.]

**88. JACK THE GIANT-KILLER.** (*c.* 1815-20). Another edition. 2*d.* plain, 3*d.* coloured. Listed in No. 92. No copy located.

**89. JOHN GILPIN, THE HISTORY OF.** By Wm. Cowper. n.d. (not later than 1808: see note below). Price 6*d.*
THE / HISTORY / OF JOHN GILPIN / OF CHEAPSIDE, / A DROLL STORY. / AND / THE HISTORICAL BALLAD, / OF THE / CHILDREN IN THE WOOD. / [vignette of the two children lost in the wood] / GLASGOW, / PUBLISHED BY LUMSDEN & SON AT THEIR / TOY BOOK MANUFAC-TORY, / PRICE SIX PENCE. / [p.s.rule]
Pp. 52. 'Illustrations'. Engraved title-page. There is a mss. inscription on the TP 'Jane Perring 1808'.
(Communicated.)
125 mm. [Ball.]

**89a. JOHN GILPIN, THE HUMOROUS HISTORY of.** [By Wm. Cowper.] n.d. (probably *c.* 1815-20). Price 6*d.*
THE HUMOROUS / HISTORY / OF / JOHN GILPIN / AND THE / HISTORICAL BALLAD / OF THE / CHILDREN IN THE WOOD / [vignette of two parents in bed, wicked uncle and two children at bedside] / GLASGOW / PUBLISHED BY J. LUMSDEN & SON. / PRICE SIXPENCE.
Pp. 52. The signatures are difficult: p. 5 is A, p. 17 is A2 and p. 21 is A3. No other pages have signatures, but the illustrations are included in the pagination although not numbered. Frontispiece of John Gilpin riding past a Public House captioned: 'Stop! Stop! John Gilpin, here's the House, they all at once did cry.' Vignette on title-page. Full page plates at pp. 8, 16, 24, 33, 41 and 49. Circular woodcut at foot of p. 51. Text: pp. 5-25, John Gilpin; pp. 25-28, Three Black Crows; pp. 28-30, Anecdotes of the Mastiff Dog; pp. 30-35, The Sagacity of the Elephant; pp. 35-48, The Children in the Wood, followed by a prose Conclusion; pp. 48-51, Dishonesty Punished; p. 52, Wise Sayings for the Use of Children.
This would appear to be a later edition of No. 89. This copy has a dated inscription on the verso of the front cover 'G. Copeman. 28th April, 1826'. The cuts appear to be of an earlier date and may well be those used in the original edition, though the title-page vignette is different. The general appearance of the volume suggests a date of 1815-20 despite the apparent earlier date of the woodcuts.
Title-page lettering is decorated with engraved scrolls. Binding: pink marbled wrappers with engraved label printed in blue on white: LUMSDEN & SON'S / NEW / EDITION / OF / JOHNNY GILPIN / & CHILDREN / IN THE / WOOD. [Within an oval design with decorative border around.] Cover label 52×68 mm. (Communicated.)
85×124 mm. Moon.

**90. KING PIPPIN.** (*c.* 1805). A Twopenny Book, listed in No. 9, perhaps an early edition of *The History of Little King Pippin,* 1814 (No. 83).

**91. LIFE . . . OF CAPTAIN WINTERFIELD, THE.** n.d. Price 6*d.*
THE / LIFE, VOYAGES, TRAVELS, / AND / WONDERFUL ADVENTURES / OF / CAPTAIN WINTERFIELD, / AN ENGLISH OFFICER, / WHO, AFTER MANY SUCCESSES AND SURPRISING ESCAPES IN EUROPE / AND AMERICA

WITH ENGLISH FORCES, BECAME, AT LAST, / A DIS-
TINGUISHED / REBEL CHIEF IN IRELAND; / INCLUD-
ING / THE BRAVERY OF A YOUNG SOLDIER, THE
PASSION OF AN ARDENT / LOVER, AND THE SKILL OF
AN INTREPID COMMANDER. / [d.p.rule] / WRITTEN BY
HIMSELF. / [d.p.rule] / [4 lines of verse] / LONDON: /
PRINTED AND SOLD BY J. BAILEY, No. 116, CHANCERY-
LANE; / SOLD ALSO BY / CHAMPANTE AND WHITROW,
ALDGATE; WILLMOTT AND HILL, BOROUGH; AND
LUMSDEN / AND SONS, GLASGOW. / [p.rule] / PRICE 6d.
In 6's [A-C⁶]. 18 leaves. Pp. 36. No illustrations.
*For notes on J. Bailey see* A curious Hieroglyphic Bible *(No. 24), the
list of books at the end of which does not include* Captain Winterfield.
*It is seldom that Lumsden's name appears in a TP imprint only as a
seller.*
Can be dated 1815-30.
181×106 mm. [BM; UCLA.]

**92. LITTLE DESERTER, THE, OR HOLIDAY SPORTS.** n.d.
(*c.* 1815-20).
THE / LITTLE DESERTER; / OR, / HOLIDAY SPORTS; / A
TALE: / DEDICATED TO ALL GOOD BOYS. / [p.rule] /
EMBELLISHED WITH ENGRAVINGS ON WOOD. / [p.rule]
/ "Gay hope is theirs, by fancy fed, / Least pleasing when
possess'd; / The tear forgot as soon as shed, / The sunshine of the
breast." — GRAY. / [p.rule] / GLASGOW: / PUBLISHED BY / J.
LUMSDEN & SON, QUEEN STREET; / AND SOLD BY JOHN
RAVEN, 6, CLEMENT'S LANE, / LONDON. [black letter] /
[PRICE 2d. PLAIN, OR 3d. COLOURED.]
Pp. [1-5], 6-29, [30-32]. 30-32 blank. 11 wood-engravings
including frontispiece, other cuts in text. Drab covers lettered
THE / LITTLE DESERTER; / OR, / HOLIDAY SPORTS. /
[p.rule] / EMBELLISHED WITH ENGRAVINGS ON WOOD.
/ [p.rule] / [woodcut] / [p.rule] / GLASGOW: / PUBLISHED BY
/ J. LUMSDEN & SON, QUEEN STREET; / AND SOLD BY
JOHN RAVEN, 6, CLEMENT'S LANE, / LONDON. / [PRICE
2d. PLAIN, OR 3d. COLOURED.] [Within a decorative
border.] Back cover advertises list of 12 titles in the series of
JUVENILE BOOKS. [Again within a decorative border.] Titles
listed are: *Whittington and his Cat*; *History of Henry Johnston*;
*Amusing Riddle Book*; *Story of Blue Beard*; *Cinderella, or Little Glass
Slipper*; *History of the Yellow Dwarf*; *Jack the Giant-Killer*; *Sleeping
Beauty in the Wood*; *The History of Robin Hood*; *History of Giles
Gingerbread*; *The Babes in the Wood*; *The Little Deserter*.

*To date this is the only title in this series located. Although some of the titles here appear in other editions it would seem that this is a separate series. For instance* Jack the Giant Killer *appears in Lumsden's Improved Edition of Coloured Twopenny Books and therefore the title listed in* The Little Deserter *must be a different issue.* (Communicated.)
115×74 mm. [NLSc.]

**LITTLE DICK.** See No. 124.

JACK CULTIVATING HIS GARDEN
AT HIS
COUNTRY SEAT

*reduced*

**93. LITTLE JACK, THE ENTERTAINING AND INSTRUCTING HISTORY OF.** By Thomas Day. n.d. (*c.* 1825-30). Price 6*d.*
Plate
THE / ENTERTAINING & INSTRUCTING / HISTORY OF /

LITTLE JACK / [d.p.rule] / EMBELLISHED WITH EIGHT ELEGANT ENGRAVINGS. / [d.p.rule] / NEW EDITION. / [vignette of the goat giving suck to the infant Jack] / GLASGOW, / PUBLISHED BY J. LUMSDEN & SON, / PRICE SIXPENCE. A single gathering of 18 leaves of text plus engraved FP and TP and 6 other engraved leaves. Of the text leaves the first is signed A, the fifth A2, the seventh A3, the ninth A4, Pp. 36.

The FP and vignette on the TP and most of the other engravings reflect John Bewick's woodcuts in Stockdale's 1788 edition of the book. This is one of the most elegant and carefully produced of Lumsden's juvenilia. The quality of the engravings, especially that on the TP is very high for books of this type. The engravings in the BM copy have been delicately coloured.

Stiff paper wrappers, pink, red, purple; pink or purple label on front wrapper: LUMSDEN & SONS / EDITION / OF / LITTLE JACK.

131×90 mm. [BM; Bondy (Cat. 79); CUL; GlaUL; MLG; NLSc; Osborne; Roscoe; Sotheby, 16 March 1970, lot 33; V & A (2 copies).]

**94. LITTLE KING PIPPIN, THE HISTORY OF.** 1814. Price 2*d.* Hugo 312.
Plate

THE / HISTORY / OF / LITTLE KING PIPPIN; / WITH / AN ACCOUNT OF THE MELANCHOLY DEATH / OF FOUR NAUGHTY BOYS, WHO WERE / DEVOURED BY WILD BEASTS; / AND / THE WONDERFUL DELIVERY OF MASTER / HARRY HARMLESS, BY A LITTLE / WHITE HORSE. / [d.p.rule] / GLASGOW: / PUBLISHED BY / J. LUMSDEN & SON. / [p.rule] / 1814.

In 8's [A-C⁸]. 24 leaves, first and last paste-downs. Pp. 47. Woodcut FP of 'Little King Pippin' and 20 very crude woodcuts in text.

Wrappers, brown, purple-brown, blue, drab. Text on upper wrapper PRICE TWOPENCE. / FROM / ROSS'S / JUVENILE / LIBRARY. / GLASGOW: / PUBLISHED BY / J. LUMSDEN & SON; on lower reversible head.

*The character 'King Pippin' derives from 'King Pepin' in the late mediaeval romance 'Valentine and Orson', but the story of the Lumsden book is entirely different from that of the romance, and is summarised in* Early Children's Books and their Illustration, *Pierpont Morgan Lib., 1975, No. 127.*

*Hugo's claim that some of the woodcuts, e.g. the Lion at p. 29, are the work of Thomas Bewick, cannot be supported, though whoever did this*

**LITTLE KING PIPPIN.**

Would you learned, good, and great?
Our Hero ſtrive to imitate;
For merit was the only thing
That made poor Pippin's ſon a King.

THE

# HISTORY

OF

## Little King Pippin;

WITH

An Account of the melancholy Death
of Four Naughty Boys, who were
devoured by Wild Beaſts;

AND

The Wonderful Delivery of MASTER
HARRY HARMLESS, by a Little
White Horſe.

GLASGOW:
Published by
J. LUMSDEN & SON.

1814.

*lion probably had Bewick's cut (by no means one of his best) in mind.
Landscapes and so on are on occasion reminiscent of early Bewick work.*
102×58 mm. [BM; GlaPL; GlaUL; MB; McEdin; NLSc; V & A.]

**95. LITTLE KING PIPPIN, THE HISTORY OF.** Gum. 3021.
The wording of the TP to this copy, as given by Gumuchian, is
approximately as for the preceding item; but it is described as
'illustrated with 15 cuts engraved on copper and printed in
bistre'. The date assigned by Gumuchian 'c. 1795' is far too early.

**96. LITTLE RED RIDING HOOD.** (c. 1805). A Penny Book,
listed in No. 9.

**LITTLE RED RIDING HOOD.** See also *Entertaining Tales of
Mother Goose* (No. 66).

**97. LONDON CRIES,** 1815. 'From Ross's Juvenile Library'. UCLA reports this as recorded by Welch. Carnan published a work of this title in 1770, another edition in 1788. (Roscoe, *Newbery J233.*)

**98. MARVELLOUS HISTORY OF MYNHEER VON WODENBLOCK, THE.** n.d. (*c.* 1815?).
THE / MARVELLOUS HISTORY / OF / MYNHEER VON WODENBLOCK. / [half-rule] / EMBELLISHED WITH / BEAUTIFUL COLOURED PLATES. / [half-rule] / GLAS-GOW: / PUBLISHED BY J. LUMSDEN & SON.
Pp. [1-5], 6, [7-8], 9-12, [13-16], 17-20, [21-22], 23-26, [27-28]. 11 hand-coloured wood-engravings, two to a page except for the frontispiece. Elaborate woodcut covers lettered LUMSDEN & SON'S / IMPROVED EDITION / OF / COLOURED / TWO-PENNY BOOKS / EMBELLISHED WITH / NUMEROUS ENGRAVINGS / MYNHEER / VON / WODENBLOCK. / [within a frame] / [emblem with 'Let Glasgow Flourish' on scroll underneath.] / LUMSDEN & SON / 20, QUEEN STREET. [The whole within a decorative frame.] Back cover advertises Coloured Prints. Price One Halfpenny. Upwards of 500 kinds. Cheap edition. Maps of every Country. Elegantly Coloured. Price 3d. only. Printed in black on grey paper. Pasted to p. 1 and 28.
(Communicated.)
123×81 mm. [NLSc.]

**99. MASTER JACKEY AND MISS HARRIOT, THE HISTORY OF.** n.d. (see note below). Price 1*d.*
THE HISTORY OF / MASTER JACKEY / AND / MISS HARRIOT. / DEDICATED TO THE / GOOD CHILDREN / OF / EUROPE, ASIA, AFRICA, AND AMERICA. / [p.rule] / [4 lines verse] / [p.rule] / PAISLEY: / PRINTED BY J. NEILSON. / AND SOLD WHOLESALE BY J. LUMSDEN / ENGRAVER, GLASGOW. / (PRICE ONE PENNY.)
Pp. 23. A number of engraved leaves. Wrappers with oval engraved portraits titled DUKE OF YORK AND DUCHESS OF YORK.
To be dated 1799 or earlier. Lumsden junior joined the firm in 1799 and is not mentioned in the imprint, where Lumsden senior is described as 'Engraver', a description given up very soon after that time.
(Communicated.)
97×61 mm. [NLSc; Welch.]

**100. MERRY ANDREW.** A twopenny edition, in or prior to 1799, was listed in *Elspy Campbell* (No. 64). There was also a twopenny edition listed in *Foundations of Learning*, *c.* 1805 (No. 9), very probably the same edition. These editions are perhaps early editions of *Fun upon Fun* (No. 72); but 'Merry Andrew' is a fairly ubiquitous character.

THE
## MERRY COBLER,
AND HIS
*MUSICAL ALPHABET.*

**GLASGOW:**
*Published and Sold Wholesale by*
J. LUMSDEN & SON.
[Price Two-pence.]

**101. MERRY COBLER, THE.** n.d. (1815-20). Price 2*d.*
Plate
THE / MERRY COBLER, / AND HIS / MUSICAL AL-PHABET. / [d.p.rule] / [Woodcut] / [d.p.rule] / GLASGOW: / PUBLISHED AND SOLD WHOLESALE BY / J. LUMSDEN & SON. / [PRICE TWO-PENCE.]
Format uncertain. 16 unsigned leaves, first and last paste-downs. Pp. 31. Woodcuts at FP, TP and p. [5], and 26 woodcuts, one for each letter of the alphabet.
The book consists of an illustrated alphabet, each with a very crude woodcut and 2 lines of feeble verse: 'I stands for Industry; / Which you see here;', 'J is a Jumper, / Without any fear.' One of

Lumsden's poorest productions, yet apparently highly success-
ful, judging by the numbers of copies (many of them well-
thumbed) now surviving.
Paper wrappers, mottled red and brown on white, yellow, pale
buff, pale grey.
91×63 mm. [Aberdeen; BCE; Bell; BM; CUL; GlaPL; GlaUL (2
copies); Hornel; MB; NLSc; OUP; Renier; Roscoe; V & A (2
copies); Welch.]

**MISS NANCY TRUELOVE, The HISTORY OF.** See *The
Friends* (No. 71).

FRONTISPIECE.

*Yellow Dwarf, p. 19.*

MOTHER BUNCH'S
𝕱𝖆𝖎𝖗𝖞 𝕿𝖆𝖑𝖊𝖘,
PUBLISHED FOR THE
AMUSEMENT
OF ALL THOSE
LITTLE MASTERS AND MISSES
WHO,
BY DUTY TO THEIR PARENTS, AND OBEDIENCE
TO THEIR SUPERIORS,
AIM AT BECOMING
*Great Lords and Ladies.*

EMBELLISHED WITH ENGRAVINGS.

GLASGOW:
PUBLISHED BY J. LUMSDEN AND SON.

[*Price Sixpence.*]

*reduced*

**102. MOTHER BUNCH'S FAIRY TALES.** By Marie
Catherine de la Mothe, Comtesse d'Aulnoy, n.d. (see note
below). Price 6*d.* Hugo 4265. NBL 432. Gum. 4205.
Plate
MOTHER BUNCH'S / FAIRY TALES. / PUBLISHED FOR
THE / AMUSEMENT / OF ALL THOSE / LITTLE MASTERS

AND MISSES / WHO, / BY DUTY TO THEIR PARENTS, AND OBEDIENCE / TO THEIR SUPERIORS, / AIM AT BECOMING / GREAT LORDS AND LADIES. / [p.rule] / EMBELLISHED WITH ENGRAVINGS. / [p.rule] / GLASGOW: / PUBLISHED BY J. LUMSDEN AND SON. / [p.rule] / [PRICE SIXPENCE.]

In 12's. [A-C¹²]. 36 leaves+6 leaves of etched plates. pp. 71. Woodcut FP (with decorative surround, captioned 'Yellow Dwarf, p. 19'). The etchings are printed in black or green and are poor work. They have nothing to do with the Bewicks, as is sometimes claimed; even Hugo had 'great doubts' as to such an attribution.

The Sotheby copy has a watermark 1817, and the book is apparently based on John Harris's edition of 1802 (Moon, *Harris* 471. It omits several of the stories in the Harris edition.

Stiff paper wrappers, purple, dark green, blue, without text. 100×85 mm. [CUL; NLSc; Osborne; Roscoe; Sotheby (22 October 1976, lot 1754); V & A (2 copies).]

## 103. MOTHER BUNCH'S FAIRY TALES. By Marie Catherine de la Mothe, Comtesse d'Aulnoy. n.d. (*c.* 1804). Price 6*d*.

Engraved TP: MOTHER BUNCH'S / FAIRY TALES / WROTE BY THE OLD WOMAN / FOR THE AMUSEMENT OF GOOD / BOYS AND GIRLS. / [d.p.rule] / EMBELLISHED WITH EIGHT ELEGANT / COPPER PLATE ENGRAVINGS. / [d.p.rule] / [engraving] / GLASGOW. / PUBLISHED BY LUMSDEN & SON AT THEIR / TOY BOOK MANUFACTORY / PRICE SIXPENCE.

(Communicated.)

[UCLA.]

## MOTHER GOOSE. See Nos. 66-70.

## 104. MOVING MARKET, THE. 1815. Price 2*d.*

THE / MOVING MARKET: / OR, / CRIES OF LONDON. / [d.p.rule] / FOR THE AMUSEMENT OF / GOOD CHILDREN. / [d.p.rule] / GLASGOW; / Published by / J. LUMSDEN & SON. / [p.rule] / 1815.

16 unsigned leaves. Pp. 31. First and last leaves paste-downs. Woodcut FP and 26 very crude woodcuts in text.

The book describes some two and a half dozen of the London

itinerant sellers of household commodities, mostly edibles. Each trade has a crude but rather attractive woodcut and four lines of verse. A book of the same title was also published by John Marshall of Aldermary Churchyard; and another by R. Marshall of the same address, price 1*d*.; this latter is described as by 'Tiffany Tarbottle'. A *Cries of London* was published by F. Newbery, Jr (1771 and later), with crude woodcuts (see Roscoe, *Newbery J86*).

BM.    Dark blue wrappers. On the upper PRICE TWOPENCE. / FROM / ROSS'S / JUVENILE / LIBRARY. / GLASGOW; / PUBLISHED BY / J. LUMSDEN & SON. On the lower a reversible head SPANIARD & JOHN BULL.

Bodley.    Grey-blue wrappers, the upper as for the BM copy, on the lower a reversible head OYSTER MAN & A FRENCH COOK.

GlaUL.    Dark green wrappers, approx, as for BM copy. Another copy has the name ROSS only on the upper cover, but is otherwise identical with the previous copy.

Shepard.    Light blue wrappers, the upper as for the BM copy; on the lower a reversible head SPANIARD & JOHN BULL.

UCLA.    On the recto of the upper wrapper is the usual FROM / ROSS'S / JUVENILE / LIBRARY. within a heart-shaped frame, and Lumsden's imprint. A woodcut of an old woman carrying a sack on the verso of the lower wrapper, used also in *Tommy Thumb's Song-Book* (No. 19).

102×63 mm. [Ball; BM; Bodley; GlaUL (2 copies); Hyde-Parker; Shepard; UCLA.]

**105. NEW CRIES OF LONDON, THE.** n.d. (*c.* 1820-30). Price 6*d.* plain, 1*s.* coloured.

Plate, and see frontispiece

THE / NEW CRIES OF / LONDON / WITH / CHARACTERISTIC ENGRAVINGS / [pictorial label of figures viewing a peepshow pasted on] / GLASGOW. / PUBLISHED BY J. LUMSDEN & SON. / PRICE SIXPENCE, PLAIN. / OR ONE SHILLING, COLOURED.

16 leaves plus covers. Pp. 34. Printed on one side of the page only. 16 engraved plates with text underneath. Lower cover has an engraving of a newsvendor displaying a news placard 'Just Published. The New Cries of London.' The engravings illustrate the following vendors: Tinker, Knifegrinder, Milkmaid, Potatoe seller, Secondhand clothes vendor, Primrose seller, Cat's Meat man, Chimney sweep, Sand seller, Chair mender, Fishmonger, Flower seller, Cherry seller, Muscle seller, Oyster seller, Watch-

man, Image seller. The fishmonger is selling mackerel.
Pink wrappers.

*This is the most expensive child's book located at the time of writing, and
seems to have been an attempt by Lumsden to enter a more lucrative
market. The fact that the engravings are printed on one side of the page
only is unusual and the pasted-on pictorial label on the front cover is
more elaborate than the usual small dignified printed label used. The
copy located is a coloured one but it is impossible to say if other similar
items in a series were ever published or whether this is an isolated attempt
at a better market which failed. It is significant no other copies have
turned up.*
(Communicated.)
122×80 mm. [MCEdin.]

NURSE DANDLEM'S

LITTLE

## 𝕽epository

OF

*GREAT INSTRUCTION*

CONTAINING

The surprising Adventures of

LITTLE WAKE WILFUL,

And his deliverance from the

*GIANT GRUMBOLUMBO.*

WRITTEN

By the Famous PRUSSIAN,

For the sole AMUSEMENT of the

*Chickabiddy Generation.*

EMBELLISHED WITH COPPERPLATES.

GLASGOW:

*Published and Sold Wholesale, by*
J. LUMSDEN and SON.

(Price Twopence.)

---

**106. NURSE DANDLEM'S LITTLE REPOSITORY OF GREAT INSTRUCTION.** n.d. (see note below). Price 2*d.* Gum. 1571-2. NBL 438. Osborne P. 28.
Plate
NURSE DANDLEM'S / LITTLE / REPOSITORY / OF / GREAT INSTRUCTION, / CONTAINING / THE SUR- PRISING ADVENTURES OF / LITTLE WAKE WILFUL, / AND HIS DELIVERANCE FROM THE / GIANT GRUMBOLUMBO. / WRITTEN / BY THE FAMOUS PRUSSIAN, / FOR THE SOLE AMUSEMENT OF THE / CHICKABIDDY GENERATION. / [wavy rule] / EMBEL- LISHED WITH COPPERPLATES. / [wavy rule] / GLASGOW: / PUBLISHED AND SOLD WHOLESALE, BY / J. LUMSDEN AND SON. / [d.p.rule] / [PRICE TWOPENCE]
The TP is on the verso of the front wrapper; the FP is on the recto of the first free leaf.
In 8's [A-B⁸]. 16 leaves of text and 8 leaves of etched plates. Pp. 47. First and last leaves paste-downs. These eight leaves are

reckoned in the pagination, but are not numbered. Small woodcuts at pp. 36 and 44. The 14 etchings are printed in sanguine.

Date about 1815. One copy seen with the watermark date 1812. Wrappers, blue, salmon pink, drab, dark brown, apricot.

100×58 mm. [Aberdeen; MBE; Bell; BM; Bodley; CUL; FlorSUL; GlaPL; GlaUL (3 copies); Hornel; MB; MLG; Moon; NLSc; NorBM; Rankin; Renier; Roscoe; Steedman (Cat. 1978); V & A (2 copies); Wood.]

**107. OBI, THE HISTORY AND ADVENTURES OF.** n.d. (*c.* 1830-40). Price 2*d.*

THE / HISTORY AND ADVENTURES / OF / OBI; / OR, / THREE-FINGERED JACK. / [p.rule] / EMBELLISHED WITH / BEAUTIFUL COLOURED PLATES. / [p.rule] / GLASGOW: / PUBLISHED BY J. LUMSDEN & SON.

14 unsigned leaves (inclusive of the wrappers). Pp. 26[27]. Coloured FP on verso of front wrapper and 10 other coloured engravings (2 to the page).

The only copy seen is in green wrappers, with an elaborate engraved text on the front wrapper LUMSDEN & SON'S / IMPROVED EDITION / OF / COLOURED / TWOPENNY BOOKS / EMBELLISHED WITH / NUMEROUS ENGRAV-INGS / OBI; / OR, / THREE-FINGERED JACK. / [coat of arms with wording 'Let Glasgow Flourish'] / LUMSDEN & SON, / 20 QUEEN STREET. There is also text on the back wrapper.

The type used and the general form of the book suggest a very late printing (up to 1850, perhaps). It does not seem to have been a success; no other edition traced, either by Lumsden or any other publisher, though 'Three-fingered Jack' sounds familiar enough, perhaps as a chapbook subject and later as a 'Penny Dreadful'.

120×80 mm. [GlaUL.]

**108. OLD DAME TROT AND HER CAT, THE HISTORY OF.** n.d.

A single sheet to decorate the nursery; 8 hand-coloured engravings each measuring *c.* 43×50 mm. Printed on one side of the leaf only. Four lines of verse below each cut. Opie suggests the cuts were also used for the poem in book form; that may well be the case.

There is no direct evidence as to dating — possibly period 1815-35. Lumsdens advertised themselves as sellers of coloured prints 'price one halfpenny; upwards of 500 kinds'.

140×224 mm. [Opie.]

**109. OLD MOTHER HUBBARD, AND HER DOG.** (? by Sarah Catherine Martin). n.d. (see notes below). Price 2*d.*
OLD / MOTHER HUBBARD, / AND / HER DOG. / [p.rule] / EMBELLISHED WITH / BEAUTIFUL COLOURED PLATES. / [p.rule] / GLASGOW: / PUBLISHED BY J. LUMSDEN & SON.
14 unsigned leaves (inclusive of front and back wrappers). Pp. 26. Coloured engraved FP on verso of front wrapper, and 10 engraved coloured plates (2 to the page).
A very late, modern type face; *c.* 1840-50.
Grey paper wrappers: LUMSDEN & SON'S / IMPROVED EDITION / OF COLOURED / TWOPENNY BOOKS / .... / LUMSDEN & SON, / 20 QUEEN STREET.
*For the history and authorship of this ancient tale see: Opie,* Three Centuries of Nursery Rhymes, *item 520; NBL, p. 59 and items 280-85; Opie,* Oxford Dictionary of Nursery Rhymes, *p. 317; and Moon,* Harris, *notes at pp. 82 and 79.*
119×80 mm. [GlaUL; Opie.]

**110. PETER MARTIN, THE HISTORY OF.** (*c.* 1820). A Halfpenny Book, listed in No. 8.

**111. PUSS IN BOOTS, THE HISTORY OF.** By Charles Perrault. n.d. Price probably 2*d.*
THE / HISTORY / OF / PUSS IN BOOTS. / [p.rule] / EMBELLISHED WITH / BEAUTIFUL COLOURED PLATES. / [p.rule] / GLASGOW: / PUBLISHED BY J. LUMSDEN & SON. [The whole within a single line border with a cross at each corner.]
26 pp. Frontispiece and 10 woodcuts on 5 leaves, all hand-coloured. The frontispiece and last page of cuts are on the verso of the covers.
Yellow printed paper wrappers, with advertisement on upper cover LUMSDEN & SON'S / IMPROVED EDITION / OF / COLOURED / TWOPENNY BOOKS / EMBELLISHED WITH / NUMEROUS ENGRAVINGS / THE STORY / OF / PUSS IN BOOTS. / [Coat of arms with wording 'Let Glasgow Flourish'.] / LUMSDEN & SON. / 20 QUEEN STREET. [The whole within a decorative border of plain rules with stars in the corners.] Lower cover identical to No. 126 where it is described in full.
120×80 mm. [BM; Wood.]

**RIQUET WITH THE TUFT.** See *Mother Goose,* Nos. 66-70.

**112. ROBIN HOOD, THE HISTORY OF.** n.d. (*c.* 1815-20).
Another edition 2*d.* plain, 3*d.* coloured. Listed in No. 92. No
copy located.

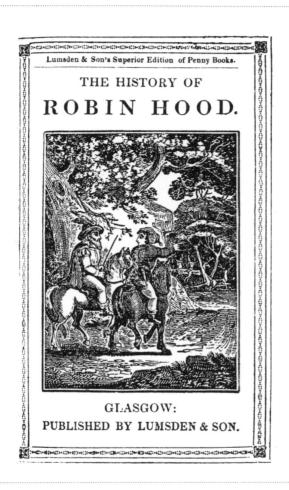

**113. ROBIN HOOD, THE HISTORY OF.** n.d. (*c.* 1830-40).
Price 1*d.*
Plate
TP on recto of front wrapper: LUMSDEN & SON'S SUPERIOR
EDITION OF PENNY BOOKS. / [p.rule] / THE HISTORY OF
/ ROBIN HOOD. / [vignette of two figures on horseback riding

along a path in the forest] / GLASGOW: / PUBLISHED BY LUMSDEN & SON. [The whole surrounded by a decorative border.]

6 unsigned leaves, inclusive of the wrappers. Pp. 11. 3 woodcuts in text.

Buff or grey wrappers; the legend on the back wrapper THE / HISTORY / OF / ROBIN HOOD etc. as for the front, but with a different woodcut. The whole within an ornamental frame. 130×80 mm. [BM; Renier.]

**114. ROBINSON CRUSOE. A SHORT SKETCH OF THE WONDERFUL LIFE OF ...** n.d. (see note below). Price 1*d*.

A / SHORT SKETCH / OF THE / WONDERFUL LIFE, / AND SURPRISING / ADVENTURES / OF THAT RENOWNED HERO, / ROBINSON CRUSOE, / WHO LIVED TWENTY-EIGHT YEARS ON AN UNIN- / HABITED ISLAND, AND WAS AFTERWARDS RELEASE- / ED BY PIRATES. / ADORNED WITH BEAUTIFUL COPPERPLATE CUTS. / [p.s.rule] / GLASGOW: / SOLD WHOLESALE BY JAMES LUMSDEN & SON. / [PRICE, ONE PENNY.]

Taken from an imperfect copy, having only the wrappers, TP and last leaf (p. 23). Beige stiff wrappers, printed in red with engraving of William and Mary and text WILLIAM AND MARY REIGNED FROM 1688 to 1702 on the front cover; engraving of George II on back with text GEORGE THE SECOND REIGNED FROM 1727-1760.

There is a mss. note 'J. J. Hoochley [or Hocchley] January 1st, 1816' on the TP; but I think the book should be dated about 1804.(S.R.)

(Communicated; no other copy traced.)

[Ries.]

**115. ROBINSON CRUSOE. THE LIFE & SURPRISING ADVENTURES OF....** n.d. (see note below). Price 6*d*.

Plate

THE / LIFE & SURPRISING / ADVENTURES OF / ROBIN-SON CRUSOE / [double rule] / EMBELLISHED WITH EIGHT ELEGANT ENGRAVINGS. / [double rule] / NEW EDITION. / [vignette of Crusoe seated on a rock in a stormy sea] / GLASGOW, / PUBLISHED BY J. LUMSDEN & SON, / PRICE SIXPENCE.

A single gathering of 18 leaves of text plus engraved FP (Crusoe finding the foot-print), engraved TP plus 6 other engraved leaves. 1st leaf of text signed A, 5th A2, 7th A3, 9th A4. Pp. 51. All leaves (including those engraved) are reckoned in the

FRONTISPIECE

*Robinson Crusoe Surprised at the mark of a human foot on the Sand.*

THE
*Life & Surprising Adventures of*
ROBINSON CRUSOE

Embellished with eight elegant Engravings.

NEW EDITION

GLASGOW,
Published by J. Lumsden & Son,

*Price Sixpence.*

*reduced*

pagination, but those engraved are unnumbered. The text is on laid paper, the engravings on wove.

Stiff paper wrappers, pink, grey-green, dark purple-brown, blue, yellow, dark green, brown. White engraved label on upper cover: LUMSDEN & SON'S / NEW / EDITION / OF / ROBINSON CRUSOE [within a diamond shaped frame].

There are watermark dates of 1818 and 1822 in copies in the Roscoe collection. The standard of production of this little book is very high indeed. He was no mere hack who did the vignette on the TP.

137×89 mm. [BM; Brimmell; Elkin Mathews (Cat. 163); GlaUL; MB; MLG; Platt; Renier (2 copies); Roscoe (2 copies); V & A (2 copies); Welch.]

**116. ROBINSON CRUSOE. THE LIFE AND SURPRISING ADVENTURES OF . . .** n.d. (catalogued as 1810).
Elkin Mathews Catalogue 163, item 107, describes a copy as in 'original marbled wrappers with engraved label . . . with FP and vignette title printed on pink paper and 6 full-page engravings'.


**117. SANDFORD AND MERTON, THE HISTORY OF.** By Thomas Day. n.d. (*c.* 1805). Price 6*d.*
Engraved TP: THE / HISTORY / OF / SANDFORD AND MERTON, / FOR THE USE OF / JUVENILE BRITONS. / [d.p.rule] / EMBELLISHED WITH EIGHT ELEGANT / COPPER PLATE PRINTS. / [d.p.rule] / [vignette, a boy chasing a butterfly with his hat] / GLASGOW. / PUBLISHED BY LUMSDEN & SON AT THEIR / TOY BOOK MANUFAC-TORY. / PRICE SIXPENCE.
*c.* 28 leaves. Pp. [2], 52. 6 whole page engraved leaves. P. [5] signed A; p. 11, A3; p. 13, B; p. 19, B3; p. 27, C3.
*First published in 1783-89, this book, in full or abridged form, went through many editions well into the 19th century, the products of many publishers. For some of the later editions see Moon,* Harris, *Nos. 192-7. It is a tedious story to prove the advantages of virtue over sin, but managed to be something of a best seller.*
(Communicated.)
[Schiller.]


**118. SELECTION OF STORIES, A. CONTAINING THE HISTORY OF THE TWO SISTERS.** n.d. (see note below). Price 6*d.* Hugo 4266. NBL. 709.
Plate
A / SELECTION OF STORIES; / CONTAINING THE HISTORY / OF THE / TWO SISTERS, / THE FISHERMAN, / THE KING AND FAIRY RING, / AND / HONESTY RE-WARDED. [d.p.rule] / EMBELLISHED WITH COPPER-PLATES. / [d.p.rule] / [p.s.rule] / GLASGOW, / PUBLISHED AND SOLD BY J. LUMSDEN & SON. / [p.rule] / PRICE SIXPENCE.
A single gathering of 24 leaves of letterpress plus engraved FP and 5 other engraved leaves, the latter reckoned in the pagination but not numbered. Of the letterpress leaves the second to the eleventh are signed A2 . . . A11. Five small woodcuts at pp. 27, 50, 51, 52, 60. Pp. 60[61]. At p. 40 a woodcut

THE PRINCE AURORA, & SHEPERDESS,
SENT to SEA by order of KING BITE

A

SELECTION OF STORIES,

CONTAINING THE HISTORY

OF THE

TWO SISTERS,

𝕮𝔥𝔢 𝔍𝔦𝔰𝔥𝔢𝔯𝔪𝔞𝔫,

THE KING AND FAIRY RING,

AND

HONESTY REWARDED.

*Embellished with Copperplates.*

GLASGOW,
Published and Sold by J. LUMSDEN & SON.

*Price Sixpence.*

*reduced*

(circular within a square frame) apes the manner of John
Bewick.
At pp. 52-53 is an oval woodcut followed by a short discourse on
'The Horse', which seems to have no connection with the rest of
the book. Mrs Sherwood's story of 'The Two Sisters' is altogether
different.
Stiff paper wrappers, blue, pink, drab. With engraved panel,
white or cream. There are watermarks 1814 and 1816.
109×82 mm. [BM; CUL; Elkin Mathews (Cat. 163); MB; NLSc;
Roscoe; V & A (2 copies); Welch.]

**119. SINBAD THE SAILOR, THE LIFE AND ADVEN-
TURES OF.** n.d. (*c.* 1805). Price 6*d.*
THE / [wavy decoration] / LIFE & ADVENTURES / OF [swelled
rule either side] / SINBAD THE SAILOR. / [Double rule] /

EMBELLISHED WITH EIGHT ELEGANT / COPPER PLATE PRINTS. / [wavy decoration] / [woodcut] / GLASGOW / PUBLISHED BY J. LUMSDEN & SON AT THEIR / TOY BOOK MANUFACTURY. / PRICE SIXPENCE. / [swelled rule].

Pp. [1-2], [1-3], 4-6, [7-8], 9-16, [17-18], 19-26, [27-28], 29-36, [37-38], 39-46, [47-48], 49-56, [57-58], 59-62. Engraved frontis. of 'Sinbad on the Whale', title-page engraving and 6 other engravings (as usual paged in). Cover in decorated pattern printed in reddish brown, reddish brown label. FINIS at foot of p. 62 followed by colophon 'LUMSDEN & SON'S JUVENILE PUBLICATIONS TO BE HAD OF / STODDART & CRAGGS, HULL.'

85×120 mm. [NLSc.]

**120. SINBAD THE SAILOR, THE LIFE AND ADVENTURES OF.** n.d. (see note below). Price 6d.

Apparently another issue of the edition above. Pp. 52. Engraved frontis., title-page and four plates of 6 (missing plates are at pp. 15/16 and pp. 42/3) included in the pagination. Signed A at p. 5, A3 at p. 11, B at p. 13, B3 at p. 19, C at p. 21 and C3 at p. 27. The first two plates are signed B and C respectively. FINIS at foot of p. 52.

Rebound in plain wrappers. Half the frontispiece is missing but part of an inscription dated '1809' is intact on verso.

115×80 mm. [Moon.]

**121. SINDBAD THE SAILOR, THE HISTORY OF.** 1819. Hugo 419.

Plate

THE / HISTORY / OF / SINDBAD, / THE SAILOR. / CONTAINING / AN ACCOUNT OF HIS SEVEN SURPRISING / VOYAGES. / [woodcut vignette of ship under sail] / GLASGOW: / PUBLISHED BY J. LUMSDEN & SON. / [wavy line] / 1819.

A single gathering of 28 leaves, the first and last 2 blanks. Woodcut FP and 7 whole-page woodcuts. Signatures at p. [5], A2; p. 9, A3; p. 13, A4; p. 17, A5; p. 19, B; p. 23, B2; p. 25, B3: The cut of the elephant at p. 48 is copied after Bewick. Some of the woodcuts (e.g. at p. 9 and p. 48) may be R. Austin's work; cf. the *Valentine's Gift*, No. 134.

Stiff paper wrappers, drab, pink, yellow. Engraved label on upper wrapper LUMSDEN & SONS, / CHILDREN'S

*Sindbad relating his Adventures.*

See p. 6, 7.

THE

# HISTORY

OF

# SINDBAD,

THE SAILOR.

CONTAINING

AN ACCOUNT OF HIS SEVEN SURPRISING

VOYAGES.

GLASGOW:

PUBLISHED BY J. LUMSDEN & SON.

1819.

*reduced*

LIBRARY. SINBAD [sic] / THE SAILOR [in a three sided ornamental frame].
135×87 mm. [GlaUL; MB; Roscoe; Sotheby (17 October 1975, lot 1244); Welch.]

**122. SINBAD THE SAILOR, THE WONDERFUL VOYAGES OF.** n.d. (1830-40). Price 2*d*.
THE / WONDERFUL VOYAGES / OF / SINBAD THE SAILOR; / BEING A HISTORY OF HIS / ASTONISHING TRAVELS, ADVENTURES, / AND SHIPWRECKS. / [p.rule] / EMBELLISHED WITH / BEAUTIFUL COLOURED

PLATES. / [p.rule] / GLASGOW: / PUBLISHED BY J. LUMSDEN & SON. [The whole within a frame of p.rules]
A single gathering of 12 leaves. The opening at pp. [8]-9 is signed B in the fold, being conjugate with pp. 20-21, the 6th and 7th leaves (conjugate) are signed C in the fold. Frontispiece and 10 woodcut illustrations on 5 leaves. All hand-coloured. The frontis. and last plate on the verso of the covers. Pp. 26. [28]. The wrappers are included in reckoning the pagination, but, with the leaves of plates, are not numbered. Upper wrapper has text LUMSDEN & SON'S / IMPROVED EDITON / OF / COL-OURED / TWOPENNY BOOKS / EMBELLISHED WITH / NUMEROUS ENGRAVINGS / VOYAGES / OF / SINBAD THE SAILOR / [Coat of Arms lettered 'Let Glasgow Flourish' underneath in a scroll] / LUMSDEN & SON, / 20 QUEEN STREET. [The whole within a ruled decorative border with stars in corners.] The lower wrapper advertises Lumsden as sellers of coloured prints 'price one halfpenny; upwards of 500 kinds', and 'maps of every country in the world elegantly coloured, price 3d only!' [The whole within identical border to upper cover.]
Paper wrappers, pale buff or pink.
120×80 mm. [Roscoe.]

*'SINBAD' and 'SINDBAD' were used indifferently.*

**123. SLEEPING BEAUTY IN THE WOOD.** (*c.* 1815-20) 2*d.* plain, 3*d.* coloured. Listed in No. 92. No copy located.

**124. STORY OF LITTLE DICK, THE.** 1823. Price 6*d.*
Plate
THE / STORY / OF / LITTLE DICK / AND / HIS PLAY-THINGS: / SHOWING / HOW A NAUGHTY BOY BECAME A GOOD ONE; / BEING AN EXAMPLE FOR ALL / LITTLE MASTERS AND MISSES / IN THE / BRITISH EMPIRE. / [p.rule] / GLASGOW: / PUBLISHED AND SOLD BY J. LUMSDEN & SON. / [wavy rule] / 1823.
A single gathering of 18 unsigned leaves, paginated [5]6-36+2 free endpapers. 8 leaves of whole page woodcuts, blank on the reverse but included in the pagination. Woodcut of a school-master and boys at p. 34 illustrating a revoltingly moral discourse 'The Contrast; or, A Picture of a Good and Bad Boy.' See a comment on this foolish story in the Introduction.

There was a pretty boy,
  Whose name was LITTLE DICK,
He long'd for every toy,
  And romp'd on grandpa's stick.

<br>

THE

# STORY

OF

# LITTLE DICK

AND

## His Playthings:

SHOWING

*How a Naughty Boy became a Good one;*

BEING AN EXAMPLE FOR ALL

LITTLE MASTERS AND MISSES

IN THE

### British Empire.

GLASGOW:

PUBLISHED AND SOLD BY J. LUMSDEN & SON.

1823.

*reduced*

Red stiff paper wrappers, the text on the upper STORY / OF /
LITTLE DICK / AND HIS / PLAYTHINGS: / SHOWING /
HOW A NAUGHTY BOY / BECAME / A GOOD ONE. /
[p.rule] / GLASGOW: / PUBLISHED AND SOLD BY J.
LUMSDEN & SON. / [wavy rule] / PRICE SIXPENCE. [The
whole within a rectangular decorated frame.] The FP woodcut is
repeated on the lower wrapper.
*One of the commoner titles, often found in pristine state suggesting an
unsold stock, but whether because of an over-optimistic printing or the
book not proving popular remains a guess.*
136×88 mm. [BCE; Bell; BM (2 copies); CUL; Elkin Mathews
(Cat. 163); FlorSUL; GlaUL; MLG; NLSc; Roscoe (2 copies).]

**125. STORY OF THE FORTY THIEVES, THE. OR, ALI BABA AND MORGIANA.** n.d. (1840-50). Price 2*d.*
THE STORY / OF / THE FORTY THIEVES; / OR, / ALI BABA AND MORGIANA. / [p.rule] / EMBELLISHED WITH / BEAUTIFUL COLOURED PLATES. / [p.rule] / GLASGOW: / PUBLISHED BY J. LUMSDEN & SON. [The whole within a frame of plain rules.]
8 unsigned leaves of text. 6 hand-coloured engraved leaves, the first and last paste-downs. Pp. 26.
Green paper wrappers with text, that on the lower wrapper reading LUMSDEN & SON'S / IMPROVED EDITION / OF COLOURED TWOPENNY BOOKS . . . ALI BABA, OR / THE FORTY THIEVES.
A very late printing.
123×82 mm. [John Johnson.]

**126. SURPRISING ADVENTURES OF TOM THUMB.** n.d. Price 2*d.*
THE / SURPRISING ADVENTURES / OF / TOM THUMB. / [p.rule] / EMBELLISHED WITH / BEAUTIFUL COLOURED PLATES. / [p.rule] / GLASGOW: / PUBLISHED BY J. LUMSDEN & SON. [The whole within a single line border with a cross at each corner.]
Pp. 26. Frontispiece and 10 woodcuts on 5 leaves, all hand-coloured. Frontis. and last plate are on the verso of the covers. White wrappers printed in black on both covers. Upper cover: LUMSDEN & SON'S / IMPROVED EDITION / OF / COLOURED / TWOPENNY BOOKS / EMBELLISHED WITH / NUMEROUS ENGRAVINGS / THE ADVENTURES / OF / TOM THUMB. / [Coat of arms with wording 'Let Glasgow Flourish'] / LUMSDEN & SON / 10 QUEEN STREET. [The whole within a decorative border.] Lower cover: LUMSDEN & SON / PUBLISHERS / OF THE / COLOURED PRINTS / PRICE ONE HALFPENNY; / UPWARDS OF 500 KINDS / THE ADVENTURES / OF / TOM THUMB. / CHEAP EDITION. / MAPS OF EVERY COUNTRY / IN THE WORLD / ELEGANTLY COLOURED. / PRICE 3d. ONLY. [Within identical border to upper cover.]
120×80 mm. [Wood.]

**127. THREE TRAVELLING COCKS, THE.** (*c.* 1820). A Halfpenny Book, listed in *Familiar Objects Described* (No. 8). It is questionable whether *The Three Travelling Cocks* be not another version of *The History of Travelling Cocks* (No. 132), though the former sold at a halfpenny, the latter at 1*d*. Until a copy of the former turns up, the question must remain open.

**128. TOBY TICKLE'S PUZZLING-CAP.** 1820. Price ½*d*.
TOBY TICKLE'S / PUZZLING-CAP. / [wavy line] / [woodcut of child holding a mask to his face] / [wavy line] / GLASGOW: / JAMES LUMSDEN AND SON. / [p.rule] / PRICE ONE HALFPENNY. [With decorative border surround.]
A single gathering of 8 unsigned leaves, including covers. Pp. 16 (numbered 4 to 15). 13 woodcuts including one on back wrapper which carries a list of 12 titles in the series. With an alphabet. The title reflects two publications of Francis Newbery, *The Hobby Horse* by Toby Ticklepitcher and *The Puzzling Cap* (Roscoe J354 and J312), both listed in 1771.
95×60 mm. [MLG.]

**129. TOM THUMB'S PLAY BOOK.** (*c.* 1805). A Penny Book, listed in No. 9.

**130. TOMMY PLAYLOVE AND JACKY LOVEBOOK, THE HISTORY OF.** 1819. (? by Stephen Jones). Price not stated, possibly 6*d*.
Plate, see page xxi
THE / HISTORY / OF / TOMMY PLAYLOVE / AND / JACKY LOVEBOOK. / WHEREIN IS SHEWN THE / SUPERIORITY OF VIRTUE OVER VICE, / HOWEVER DIGNIFIED BY BIRTH OR FORTUNE. / [wavy rule] / EMBELLISHED WITH ELEGANT CUTS. / [d.p.rule] / GLASGOW: / PUBLISHED BY J. LUMSDEN & SON. / [wavy rule] / 1819.
A single gathering of 26 leaves, the 3rd signed A2, 5th A3, 7th A4, 9th A5, 10th B, 12th B2, 13th B3, pp. 51. Woodcut frontispiece, and 12 circular woodcuts in text, these being in the manner of John Bewick or Lee.
Stiff paper or card wrappers, drab, pink. Yellow or pink label on front wrapper: LUMSDEN & SONS / EDITION OF / TOMMY PLAYLOVE / & JACKY LOVEBOOK [within a frame].
*First published by E. Newbery in 1783 (Roscoe, Newbery J189). The attribution to Stephen Jones is not definite; see Moon, Harris, Nos. 403 and 405.*
137×88 mm. [BM (with hand-coloured woodcuts); GlaUL; Gross (Cat. 25); NLSc; Osborne; Schiller (Cat. 29); V & A (2 copies).]

**131. TOMMY TRIP'S VALENTINE GIFT.** n.d. (*c.* 1800). Price 1*d.*

TOMMY TRIP'S / VALENTINE GIFT: / A PLAN TO ENABLE CHILDREN OF ALL / SIZES AND DENOMINA- TIONS / TO BEHAVE WITH / HONOUR, INTEGRITY, AND HUMANITY. / TO WHICH IS ADDED, / SOME ACCOUNT OF OLD ZIGZAG, AND OF / THE HORN WHICH HE USED TO UNDERSTAND / THE LANGUAGE OF BIRDS, BEASTS, / FISHES, AND INSECTS. / ADORNED WITH COPPERPLATES. / PAISLEY: / PRINTED BY J. NEILSON, / AND SOLD WHOLESALE BY J. LUMSDEN, / ENGRAVER, GLASGOW. / [PRICE ONE PENNY.]

Pp. [1-3], 4-15, [16]. There are four engraved plates each with two subjects printed in rose pink and not paged in. Engraved cover showing Princess and Prince of Wales in black stuck to outside of pp. [1] and [16].

*Vol. 2 of the Osborne Catalogue (at p. 950) assumes that the book was in fact* The Valentine's Gift *(see No. 134) and lists an edition under the title* Tommy Trip's Valentine Gift *published by Osborne & Griffin and Mozley, Gainsborough in 1785. 'Tommy Trip' and 'Valentine's Gift' were probably both the invention of John Newbery.* (Communicated.)

100×80 mm. [NLSc.]

**132. TRAVELLING COCKS, THE HISTORY OF.** n.d. (*c.* 1830-40). Price 1*d.*

Plate

TP on recto of front wrapper: LUMSDEN AND SON'S SUPERIOR / EDITION OF PENNY BOOKS. / [p.rule] / THE / HISTORY / OF / TRAVELLING / COCKS. / [p.rule] / [woodcut of large cockerel with farmyard background] / [p.rule] / GLASGOW: / PUBLISHED BY / LUMSDEN & SON. [The whole within a frame.]

6 unsigned leaves, inclusive of the wrappers. Pp. 11. 5 woodcuts in the text, flanked by printer's ornaments. Woodcut at p. 8 signed 'Kelly'. The woodcut on the title-page is almost certainly copied (or derived) from Bewick's woodcut of this subject in his *History of British Birds*, 1797, vol. I, p. 274. The cuts are of unusually high standard.

The legend on the back wrapper THE / HISTORY / OF / TRAVELLING / COCKS etc. as for the front, but with a different woodcut. [The whole within a frame.]

*It is questionable whether this book is another edition of* The Three

Travelling Cocks *(see note to No. 127), but advertisements were not over accurate in this respect.*
130×79 mm. [BM.]

**133. TRIUMPH OF GOODNATURE, THE.** n.d. (*c.* 1818-20).
Price 6*d.* Hugo 314. NBL 710.
Plate
THE / TRIUMPH OF GOODNATURE, / EXHIBITED IN THE / HISTORY / OF / MASTER HARRY FAIRBORN, / AND / MASTER TRUEWORTH. / INTERSPERSED WITH / TALES AND FABLES. / [d.p.rule] / EMBELLISHED WITH

THE

## TRIUMPH OF GOODNATURE,

EXHIBITED IN THE

## HISTORY

OF

### 𝔐aster 𝔥arry 𝔉airborn,

AND

## MASTER TRUEWORTH.

INTERSPERSED WITH

TALES AND FABLES.

EMBELLISHED WITH ELEGANT CUTS.

GLASGOW:

Published and Sold by J. LUMSDEN & SON.

*Price Sixpence.*

*reduced*

ELEGANT CUTS. / [d.p.rule] / [p.s.rule] / GLASGOW: / PUBLISHED AND SOLD BY J. LUMSDEN & SON. / [wavy rule] / PRICE SIXPENCE.

In 6's [A-F⁶], the last blank. 38 leaves, being 35 leaves of text and woodcuts plus one endpaper at the beginning, one blank leaf of text and one endpaper at end. Pp. 70. Woodcut FP and 13 other whole page cuts.

The watermark $\frac{C}{25}$ is on two of the blanks. A copy sold at Sotheby's Oct. 13th, 1977, lot 2554, was watermarked 1818.

Stiff paper wrappers, red with engraved orange label on upper cover LUMSDEN & SONS / EDITION / OF / THE TRIUMPH / OF GOODNATURE [within a frame]. Labels also dark green, dark red, grey-blue, yellow, pink and yellow.

*This story is not in the normal mould, lacking as it does most of the usual dreary contrasting between good and bad children; they are all quite reasonably and pleasantly human. The principal characters, Harry Fairborn and Master Trueworth, end up most satisfactorily (with names like that they could scarcely do otherwise): 'Master Fairborn . . . was provided with such a place in London, and in time so well promoted, that he became at last as rich as Sir Charles himself, and lived to be the comfort of his parents, and to see Master Trueworth and all his friends happy.'*

133×86 mm. [CUL; GlaUL; Maxwell Hunley (Cat. 48); NLSc; Roscoe; V & A (3 copies); Welch.]


**TWO SISTERS, THE FISHERMAN, THE KING AND FAIRY RING, AND HONESTY REWARDED.** See *Selection of Stories* (No. 118).


**134. VALENTINE'S GIFT, THE.** n.d. (1816 or after). Price 6*d.* Hugo 311.

Plate

THE / VALENTINE'S GIFT; / OR, / A PLAN / TO ENABLE CHILDREN OF ALL DENOMINATIONS TO BEHAVE WITH / HONOUR, INTEGRITY, AND HUMANITY. / TO WHICH IS ADDED, / SOME ACCOUNT OF OLD ZIGZAG, / AND OF THE HORN WHICH HE USED / TO UNDERSTAND THE LANGUAGE OF / BIRDS, BEASTS, FISHES, AND / INSECTS. / [p.rule] / [3 line quote . . . Zoroaster.] / [p.rule] / GLASGOW: / PUBLISHED AND SOLD BY J. LUMSDEN & SON. / [wavy rule] / PRICE SIXPENCE.

In 6's [A-F⁶]. 36 leaves, the first and last paste-downs. Pp. 67. Woodcut FP and 14 other whole page woodcuts, those at pp. 34 and 39 signed 'R. Austin'; the others are probably by him.

The watermark date 1816 appears in the Roscoe copy at F2.

*For the possible identity of this with* Tommy Trip's Valentine Gift *(No. 131) see the note on the latter at p. 950 of the Osborne Cat. Vol. II. First published by John Newbery in 1764 or 1765 (Roscoe, Newbery J368). Mr Simpson discourses to his wife and children on Valentine's Day customs and this leads to accounts of what birds and beasts say to each other according to 'old Zigzag', though Mr Simpson, miserable kill-joy that he is, warns that these stories are not to be believed, as 'these things are unknown to us'. The story is liberally strewn with references to other tales published by John Newbery though he is not named.*

THE

## 𝕍alentine's Gift;

or,

## A PLAN

To enable Children of all Denominations to behave with

HONOUR, INTEGRITY, AND HUMANITY.

TO WHICH IS ADDED,

### Some account of Old Zigzag,

AND OF THE HORN WHICH HE USED

To understand the Language of

### *Birds, Beasts, Fishes, and Insects.*

*The Lord who made thee, made the creatures also; thou shalt be merciful and kind unto them, for they are thy fellow tenants of the globe.*

ZOROASTER.

### GLASGOW:
Published and Sold by J. LUMSDEN & SON.

*Price Sixpence.*

reduced

Stiff paper wrappers, drab, blue, yellow, red. With an engraved label on the upper, LUMSDEN & SONS / EDITION / OF / VALENTINE'S GIFT [within an ornamental frame]. The label brown yellow, purple or pink.
136×86 mm. [BM; CUL; GlaPL; GlaUL; MB; NLSc; Renier; Roscoe; Sotheby (4 March 1977, lot 474); V & A.]

**135. WAGGON LOAD OF AMUSEMENT, THE.** n.d. (*c.* 1830-40). Price 1*d.* Hugo 4272.
TP on recto of front wrapper: LUMSDEN & SON'S SUPERIOR EDITION OF PENNY BOOKS, / [p.rule] / THE / WAGGON LOAD / OF / AMUSEMENT. / [p.rule] / [vignette] / [p.rule] /

GLASGOW: / PUBLISHED BY LUMSDEN & SON. [The whole within an ornamental framed decoration of foliage.] 6 unsigned and unnumbered leaves, inclusive of the wrappers. Pp. 11. 21 woodcuts in text, flanked by printer's ornaments. The legend on the back wrapper THE / WAGGON LOAD etc. as for the front, but with a different woodcut. [The whole within an ornamental frame.] 129×78 mm. [BM.]

**136. THE WAY TO BE HAPPY.** By A.M. 1819. Price not stated, probably 6*d.* Hugo 417. Gum. 1565. CBEL, II, 1026. Plate

THE / WAY TO BE HAPPY: / OR, / THE HISTORY / OF THE / FAMILY AT SMILEDALE. / TO WHICH IS ADDED, / THE STORY OF LITTLE GEORGE. / [p.s.rule] / GLASGOW: / PUBLISHED BY J. LUMSDEN & SON. / [wavy rule] / 1819. Two gatherings of 18 and 6 leaves, the 5th, 7th and 9th leaves of the 1st signed A2, A3, A4; the first 3 leaves of the 2nd signed B, B2, B3. Pp. 47. Blanks at beginning and end. Woodcut FP and 12 circular woodcuts within a rectangular frame for *The Way to Be Happy* and the following four stories. These are copies in reverse after the cuts by, or in close imitation of John Bewick used in the earlier editions by E. Newbery and John Harris. (Roscoe. J235 and Moon. 508.) It seems most probable the text is, or derives from Newbery. Three woodcuts for *Little George*, oval within a frame, are very poor work. That at p. 41 is adapted from the cut for the fable of 'The Elephant and the Bookseller' in T. Saint's 1779 edition of Gay's *Fables*, or one of its later versions. Stiff paper wrappers, drab, violet-pink, pink, with engraved label on upper cover, LUMSDEN & SONS / EDITION / OF THE / SMILEDALE FAMILY [within a frame], the label brown, pink, yellow, red.

*The letter of dedication to 'Mrs. Teachwell' (i.e. Lady Eleanor Fenn) in the Newbery edition is signed 'A.M.' See Roscoe, Newbery J235. Romer recorded an edition of 1818 in his Catalogue No. 52. This is almost certainly an error for 1819, as he quotes Hugo 417.*

In addition to The Way to be Happy *and* Little George *mentioned in the title-page, the work includes* The Honest Tar, The History of Sweet-Pea, The Adventures of Henry Lily, The Story of Little Echo. *These additional stories are not in the Newbery edition.* The Way to be Happy *is a very brief story about Francesca, a happy little girl who lives at Smiledale, and is invited to visit her Godmother. They walk in the garden where the Godmother orates on the Gum-Cistus*

THE SMILEDALE FAMILY.

THE

# WAY TO BE HAPPY:

OR,

## THE HISTORY

OF THE

### FAMILY AT SMILEDALE.

TO ,WHICH IS ADDED,

**THE STORY OF LITTLE GEORGE.**

————

GLASGOW:

PUBLISHED BY J. LUMSDEN & SON.

1819.

*reduced*

*and quotes some verses to be worked into a sampler by Francesca.*
138×89 mm. [CUL; FlorSUL; GlaUL; Maxwell Hunley (Cat. 48); MB; NLSc; Roscoe; UCLA; V & A.]

**137. WHITTINGTON AND HIS CAT.** (*c.* 1805). A Penny Book, listed in No. 9.

**138. WHITTINGTON AND HIS CAT.** (*c.* 1815-20). 2*d.* plain, 3*d.* coloured. Listed in No. 92. No copy located.

**139. WHITTINGTON AND HIS CAT, THE HISTORY OF.** (*c.* 1820). A Halfpenny Book, listed in No. 8.

**140. WHITTINGTON AND HIS CAT.** n.d. (*c.* 1830-40, see note below). Price 1*d.*
Plate
TP on recto of front wrapper: LUMSDEN AND SON'S SUPERIOR EDITION OF PENNY BOOKS. / WHITTING-TON / AND HIS CAT. / [large woodcut] / [p.rule] / GLASGOW: / PUBLISHED BY LUMSDEN & SON. [The whole within an ornamental frame.]
6 unsigned leaves, inclusive of the wrappers. Pp. 11. 6 woodcuts in text.
Green wrappers; the legend on the back wrapper THE HISTORY / OF / WHITTINGTON / AND HIS CAT. etc. as for

the front, but with a different woodcut. [The whole within an ornamental frame.]

*The early nineteenth century produced a crop of editions of this very ancient story, which was in print before 1605. See the Osborne* Catalogue *and Moon's* Harris.

130×76 mm. [BM.]

**141. WILLIAM AND HIS DOG.** *c.* 1820. Price ½*d.*

WILLIAM / AND / HIS DOG. / [wavy rule] / [woodcut of William showing the dog to his father] / [wavy rule] / GLASGOW: / JAMES LUMSDEN AND SON. / [p.rule] / PRICE ONE HALFPENNY. [Within a decorative border.]

A single gathering of 8 unsigned leaves, including covers. Pp. 16 (numbered 6 to 15). With 12 woodcuts including one on back wrapper with list of titles in the series underneath. One of the cuts is a repeat of the one used on the front cover. With an alphabet. Of the four titles examined in this series this is the only one to have a cut labelled 'frontispiece', and a tailpiece cut labelled 'finis'. Note cover title differs from the advertisements of title with omission of word 'Little'. Full title is used at beginning of text.

97×59 mm. [MLG.]

**WINTERFIELD, CAPTAIN.** See No. 91.

**142. WONDERS OF A DAY.** (*c.* 1805). A Twopenny Book, listed in No. 9.

**143. YELLOW DWARF, THE HISTORY OF THE.** (*c.* 1815-20). 2*d.* plain, 3*d.* coloured. Listed in No. 92. No copy located.

# 6
# CHAPBOOKS

## CHAPBOOK AUTHORITIES REFERRED TO IN THIS LIST

LAURISTON: *The Catalogue of the Lauriston Castle Chapbooks in the National Library of Scotland.* G. K. Hall & Co., Mass. USA. 1964.

FAIRLEY: John A. Fairley. *Dougal Graham & the Chapbooks by and attributed to him with a bibliography.* J. Maclehose & Sons, Glasgow. 1914.

# A NOTE ON THE CHAPBOOKS

The Chapbooks listed here form a striking contrast with the books for children, religious works and so on in Lists 1 to 5, which could be read in the family circle of the better educated, 'without bringing a blush to the cheek of modesty'. Of some at least of these Chapbooks that certainly could not be said.

The Chapbooks published by Lumsdens were Chapbooks proper, the little cheap books hawked about the country by the chapmen, not what is now coming to be the accepted meaning of the word: any very small, elderly book usually meant for juvenile readers. Under that meaning most of the books in the preceding lists would be 'chapbooks'.

The chapman's chief customers were the farming communities, the shepherds, the labourers in remote parts of the country where there were no bookshops. Often they were living at near starvation level, or at all events with not more than a penny or two to spend now and then on the luxury of a book. Hence it came about that the books sold by the chapmen had to be brief, without any of the refinements of book-production which would in any way increase costs, roughly printed on the coarsest and cheapest paper, without wrapper or cover of any sort, and almost always the entire book printed on a single sheet. Many of these chapbooks were printed for Lumsden by Neilson of Paisley, and it is interesting to note that whereas the bulk of Lumsdens' other publications were undated, the reverse applied here, only some half dozen of their chapbooks bearing no date.

F. W. Ratcliffe, in his paper *Chapbooks with Scottish Imprints in the Robert White Collection. . . . Newcastle on Tyne* (The Bibliotheck, Vo. 4, 1963-6, at p. 92), says 'The obvious characteristic of the Chapbook is that it is contained in the sheet. It belongs to the same tradition as the broadsheet, not with the signed sections of a book. It may appear in twos, fours, sixes, eights, tens, twelves, but it should not exceed one sheet.' A chapbook was seldom enlivened with more than one woodcut; any old cut would do whether or not relevant to the text. Thus, for example, the bust of a Roman Emperor was scarcely appropriate to *The Comical Transactions of Lothian Tom* (No. 149), or *The Witty and entertaining Exploits of George Buchanan* (No. 171), but there it is on the title-pages, for all to see, and presumably, appreciate. Sometimes there were no woodcuts at all, sometimes the impression of cuts were from blocks so old and cracked as to be almost unintelligible.

So in the course of time the chapbook came to have its own standard format and appearance: between two and twelve leaves in a single sewing, the untrimmed paper, rough and grey, at once recognisable by potential buyers as the stuff of their choice, to be read aloud of an evening, where the community had a literate member, and often consisting of matter which, to the present-day ear, is either utter stupidity (witness *The Comical Sayings of Paddy from Cork* (No. 148)) or black indecency, either of which might well set the listeners in a roar. Of course there were sober books too, *The Life of Sir William Wallace* (No. 160), Allan Ramsay's *Collection of Scots Proverbs* (Nos. 145-6) (there were two editions of this), and so on.

Twenty of the twenty-seven chapbooks here recorded have woodcuts on the title-pages. Of these cuts five were used twice and these almost inevitably show marks of long usage and rough handling. Most, if not all of them are a good deal older than the books they decorate. Lumsdens were not spending a penny on new cuts for books which sold retail for a very few pence, if it could be avoided, as it usually was.

The firm's output of chapbooks was very small when set against the vast numbers recorded in Lauriston, and the great holdings in the British Library, the Robert White collection at Newcastle, and elsewhere. A catalogue recently published by an eminent firm of booksellers, comprising 'Battledores, Chapbooks and Pamphlets . . . originally published at sixpence or less' and arranged in order of the places of publication, lists about 96 of these items published in Glasgow, the majority 'by the Booksellers' and dated *c.* 1840. Not a single one of these was published by the Lumsdens. The period of the firm's activities in this branch of publishing, extended, on present information, only from 1816 to 1822, with one of doubtful date (owing to broken digits, but probably 1822), and excluding the 1808 chapbook *The Unfortunate Lovers* (No. 169). The dates and numbers issued were 1816 one, 1817 two, 1820 five, 1821 three, 1822 (the climax) eight. There were six undated books which I assign to this period. It seems clear enough that Lumsdens were not able to work up a worth-while connection in this line, a line already amply supplied by the publishers of London, Paisley, Edinburgh and elsewhere. And although the lines of publishing did in theory, widen Lumsden's market, catering for the poor as well as the well-to-do, it may have brought them into some disfavour with the better educated class of buyers, who would not think well of a firm which could turn out stupidity and dirt, along with epitomes of the Bible and Watts' *Divine Songs*.

**144. BATTLE OF CHEVY-CHACE, THE.** 1821. Lauriston, 2844.A.(18).
THE / BATTLE / OF / CHEVY-CHACE. / AN / EXCELLENT OLD BALLAD. / [woodcut] / GLASGOW; / PUBLISHED BY J. LUMSDEN & SON. / [p.rule] / 1821.
8vo. 4 unsigned leaves. Pp. 8. No woodcuts in text.
*An immensely popular work. Lauriston lists twenty-four editions. The B.M catalogue about the same.*
(Communicated.)
160×95 mm. [NLSc; St. Andrews.]

**145. COLLECTION OF SCOTS PROVERBS, A.** By Allan Ramsay. 1820. Lauriston 2844 (9).
Plate
A / COLLECTION / OF / SCOTS PROVERBS, / CONSISTING OF THE / WISE SAYINGS AND OBSERVATIONS / OF THE / OLD PEOPLE OF SCOTLAND. / [p.rule] / BY ALLAN RAMSAY, / THE SCOTS POET. / [p.rule] / VOX POPULI VOX DEI. / THAT MAUN BE TRUE THAT A' MEN SAY. / [woodcut of crown and thistle] / GLASGOW: / PUBLISHED BY J. LUMSDEN & SON. / [p.rule] / 1820.
12 unsigned leaves. Pp. [1,2] 3-24. No woodcuts in text.
(Communicated.)
171×97 mm. [NLSc.]

**146. COLLECTION OF SCOTS PROVERBS, A.** By Allan Ramsay. 1821. Lauriston 2844 (10).
Another edition of above, the type reset, otherwise identical.
(Communicated.)
167×99 mm. [NLSc.]

**147. COMICAL HISTORY OF SIMPLE JOHN, THE.** n.d.
Attributed to Dougal Graham.
Plate
THE / COMICAL HISTORY / OF / SIMPLE JOHN, / AND HIS / TWELVE MISFORTUNES, / WHICH HAPPENED ALL IN TWELVE DAYS AFTER THE / UNHAPPY DAY OF HIS MARRIAGE. / GIVING A PARTICULAR ACCOUNT OF HIS COURTSHIP AND MARRIAGE / TO A SCOLDING WIFE: WHICH HAS BEEN A MORTIFYING / MISERY TO MANY A POOR MAN. / O SIRS WILL YOU SEE / WHAT IT IS TO MARRY'D BE! / [woodcut] / GLASGOW: / PUBLISHED BY J. LUMSDEN & SON.
4 unsigned leaves. Pp. 8. Text begins on verso of title-leaf. No

A

# COLLECTION

OF

# SCOTS PROVERBS,

CONSISTING OF THE

*Wise Sayings and Observations*

OF THE

OLD PEOPLE OF SCOTLAND.

By ALLAN RAMSAY,

THE SCOTS POET.

VOX POPULI VOX DEI.

*That maun be true that a' Men say.*

GLASGOW:

Published by J. LUMSDEN & SON.

1820.

THE

# COMICAL HISTORY

OF

# SIMPLE JOHN,

AND HIS

## Twelve Misfortunes,

Which happened all in Twelve Days after the
unhappy Day of his Marriage.

Giving a particular account of his Courtſhip and Marriage
to a Scolding wife: which has been a mortifying
miſery to many a Poor Man.

*O ſirs will you see*
*What it is to Marry'd be !*

GLASGOW:
Published by J. LUMSDEN & SON.

THE

## COMICAL TRANSACTIONS

OF

# LOTHIAN TOM.

### IN SIX PARTS.

Wherein is contained a Collection of Ro-
guifh Exploits done by him both in
Scotland and England.

## GLASGOW:

Publifhed by J. Lumsden & Son.

## 1820.

*149*: The Comical Transactions of Lothian Tom.

woodcuts in text. The TP woodcut is also used in *The History of John Cheap* (No. 156).
*A popular subject. Lauriston lists some thirteen editions.*
(Communicated.)
150×85 mm. [Aberdeen.]

### 148. COMICAL SAYING OF PADDY FROM CORK, THE. 1822.
THE / COMICAL SAYING / OF / PADDY FROM CORK. / WITH HIS COAT BUTTONED BEHIND, / BEING AN ELEGANT CONFERENCE BETWEEN ENGLISH TOM AND / IRISH TEAGUE; WITH PADY'S [sic] CATECHISM, HIS OPINION / OF PURGATORY, THE STATE OF THE DEAD; AND HIS SUP- / PLICATION WHEN A MOUN-TAIN SAILOR, / ALSO, / A CREDE FOR ALL ROMISH BELIEVERS. / [p.rule] / IN ALL ITS PARTS, CARE-FULLY CORRECTED. / [p.rule] / [woodcut] / GLASGOW, / PUBLISHED BY J. LUMSDEN & SON. / [p.rule] / 1822.
(Communicated.)
164×88 mm. [UCLA (only the TP has survived).]

### 149. COMICAL TRANSACTIONS OF LOTHIAN TOM, THE. 1820. Attributed to Dougal Graham. Lauriston, p. 110. Fairley, 62.
Plate
THE / COMICAL TRANSACTIONS / OF / LOTHIAN TOM. / [p.rule] / IN SIX PARTS / [p.rule] / WHEREIN IS CON-TAINED A COLLECTION OF RO- / GUISH EXPLOITS DONE BY HIM BOTH IN / SCOTLAND AND ENGLAND. / [woodcut] / GLASGOW: / PUBLISHED BY J. LUMSDEN & SON. / [p.rule] / 1820.
The TP is on the recto of the upper wrapper. A single gathering of 12 unsigned leaves. Pp. 24 Woodcut of a bull at p. 24. The TP woodcut also used in No. 171. 'J. Neilson, printer' at foot of p. 24.
*A singularly coarse production, of which there were several editions.*
162×97 mm. [BM; NLSc; Roscoe.]

### 150. EXCELLENT OLD SONG, AN. 1821.
AN EXCELLENT OLD SONG, / INTITLED / YOUNG BEICHAN / AND / SUSIE PYE. / TO WHICH IS ADDED, / BRITANNIA'S CALL. / [woodcut] / GLASGOW: PUBLISHED BY J. LUMSDEN & SON. / [p.rule] / 1821.
Pp. [1-2], 3-8. Imprint J. Neilson, printer on p. 8.
(Communicated.)
145×98 mm. [NLSc.]

AN EXCELLENT

SONG,

ENTITLED,

# ROSANNA;

OR,

## THE OXFORD TRAGEDY.

GLASGOW:
Published by J. Lumsden & Son.

1821.

*151*: An Excellent Song, entitled, Rosanna.

**151. EXCELLENT SONG, ENTITLED, ROSANNA; OR, THE OXFORD TRAGEDY, AN.** 1821.
Plate
AN EXCELLENT / SONG, / ENTITLED, / ROSANNA; / OR, / THE OXFORD TRAGEDY. / [woodcut] / GLASGOW: / PUBLISHED BY J. LUMSDEN & SON. / [p.rule] / 1821.
4 unsigned leaves. Pp. 8. The TP woodcut is also used in No. 161. (Communicated.)
169×114 mm. [St. Andrews.]

**152. FUN UPON FUN! OR, THE COMICAL MERRY TRICKS OF LEPER THE TAYLOR.** In Two Parts. 1817.
Attributed to Dougal Graham. Fairley 99. Lauriston 3062 (p. 107).
FUN UPON FUN! / OR, THE / COMICAL MERRY TRICKS / OF / LEPER THE TAYLOR. / [p.rule] / IN TWO PARTS / [p.rule] / TO WHICH ARE ADDED, / THE / GRAND SOLEMNITY OF THE TAYLOR'S FUNERAL, / WHO LAY / NINE NIGHTS IN STATE ON HIS OWN SHOP BOARD. / TOGETHER WITH HIS / LAST WILL & TESTAMENT. / [woodcut] / GLASGOW: / PUBLISHED BY J. LUMSDEN & SON. / [p.rule] / 1817.
12 unsigned leaves. Pp. 24. No woodcuts in text. Imprint of J. Neilson, printer at foot of p. 24. The woodcut on the title-page was also used on the title to *The Laird of Cool's Ghost* (No. 159). *This chapbook is no relative of the Lumsden juvenile with the same title (No. 72), but the title was obviously an attractive one, and both works appear to have been brisk sellers. Lauriston records some 18 editions of the chapbook. Another edition by Lumsden is* The Merry Tricks of Leper the Taylor (*No. 165*).
156×93 mm. [BM; NLSc.]

**GIG DEMOLISHED, THE.** See Nos. 167 and 168.

**153. HISTORY OF BUCHAVEN IN FIFESHIRE, THE.** 1821.
THE / HISTORY OF BUCHAVEN / IN FIFESHIRE, / CONTAINING THE WITTY AND ENTERTAINING / EXPLOITS OF WISE WILLIE / AND / WITTY EPPY, / [woodcut] / THE ALE WIFE, / WITH A DESCRIPTION OF THEIR COLLEGE, COATS OF ARMS, &c. / [p.rule] / ADORNED WITH WOOD CUTS. / [p.rule] / GLASGOW; / PUBLISHED BY J. LUMSDEN & SON. / [p.rule] / 1821.
12 unsigned leaves. Pp. 24. [4-24]. Imprint of J. Neilson at foot of p. 24. Woodcuts on [p. 3.] 4, 6, 8, 9, 11, 16, 18, 23, 24. i.e. 11 including the TP cut.
The only copy examined had been bound up and interleaved. A

# THE HISTORY

OF

## Duncan Campbell,

AND HIS

## DOG, OSCAR.

*FROM HOGG'S EVENING TALES.*

GLASGOW:

Publifhed by J. Lumsden & Son.

## 1822.

*154*: The History of Duncan Campbell.

THE

# HISTORY

OF

# JACK AND THE GIANTS,

IN ALL ITS PARTS.

CONTAINING

I. *Jack's birth and parentage, his dispute with a Country Vicar, &c.*

II. *How he slew a Monstrous Giant on the Mount of Cornwall, & was called Jack the Giant Killer*

III. *How King Arthur's son met with Jack, and what happened.*

IV. *How Jack saved his master's life, drove the evil spirits out of a Lady, &c.*

V. *A full account of his victorious conquests over the North Country Giants, how he destroyed the enchanted castle kept by Galligantus; dispersed the fiery griffins; put the Conjuror to flight; released many Knights and Ladies, likewise a Duke's daughter, to whom he was married with many more of his Adventures.*

G L A S G O W:
PUBLISHED BY J. LUMSDEN & SON

### 1822.

*155*: The History of Jack and the Giants.

THE

# HISTORY

OF

# JOHN CHEAP,

*THE CHAPMAN.*

CONTAINING

Above a Hundred Merry Exploits done by him and his Fellow Traveller, DROUTHY TOM, a fticked Shaver.

## IN THREE PARTS.

GLASGOW :

Publifhed by J. LUMSDEN & SON.

1820.

*156*: The History of John Cheap, the Chapman.

previous owner had written on the title-page 'One of three copies printed on large paper'. This seems to be a piece of wishful thinking on his part — it is merely untrimmed with each leaf slightly different in size.

175×120 mm. [MLG; Sotheby (1 March 1978, lot 133A).]

**154. HISTORY OF DUNCAN CAMPBELL, AND HIS DOG, OSCAR, THE.** Lauriston 2844 (12).
Plate
THE HISTORY / OF / DUNCAN CAMPBELL, / AND HIS / DOG, OSCAR. / FROM HOGG'S EVENING TALES. / [woodcuts of man and his dog] / GLASGOW: / PUBLISHED BY J. LUMSDEN & SON. / [p.rule] / 1822.
12 unsigned leaves. Pp. [1,2] 3-24. No woodcuts in text.
The figure of the man in the larger of the two woodcuts on the TP almost without doubt derives from the frontispiece to *A Collection of Pretty Poems for . . . Children six foot high*, published by John Newbery in 1757 and later (Roscoe, *Newbery* J74). (Communicated.)
165×99 mm. [NLSc.]

**155. HISTORY OF JACK AND THE GIANTS, THE.** 1822.
Plate
THE / HISTORY / OF / JACK AND THE GIANTS. / [p.rule] / IN ALL ITS PARTS. / [p.rule] / CONTAINING / [Parts and list of contents — 15 lines] / GLASGOW: / PUBLISHED BY J. LUMSDEN & SON. / [p.rule] / 1822.
12mo. 12 unsigned leaves. Pp. 24. No woodcuts.
156×88 mm. [GlaUL.]

**156. HISTORY OF JOHN CHEAP, THE CHAPMAN, THE.** 1820. Attributed to Dougal Graham. Lauriston, 2844(5), p. 110. Fairley 83.
Plate
THE / HISTORY / OF / JOHN CHEAP, / THE CHAPMAN. / CONTAINING / ABOVE A HUNDRED MERRY EXPLOITS DONE BY / HIM AND HIS FELLOW TRAVELLER, DROUTHY / TOM, A STICKED SHAVER. / IN THREE PARTS / [woodcut] / GLASGOW: / PUBLISHED BY J. LUMSDEN & SON. / 1820.
12 unsigned leaves. Pp. 24. Imprint of J. Neilson, printer, at foot of p. 24. No woodcuts in text. The TP woodcut used also in *The Comical History of Simplejohn* (No. 147).
*A popular title. Lauriston lists some 11 editions and issues.*
165×93 mm. [BM; NLSc.]

# THE
# Laird of Cool's
# GHOST!

**BEING**

A Copy of several Conferences and Meetings that
past betwixt the Rev. Mr. Ogilvie, late Minister of
the Gospel at Innerwick in East Lothian, and the
Ghost of Mr. Maxwell, late Laird of Cool.

As it was found in Mr. Ogilvie's closet after his Death,
very soon after these Conferences.

[WRITTEN BY HIS OWN HAND.]

GLASGOW:
PUBLISHED BY J. LUMSDEN & SON.

**157. HISTORY OF THE WICKED LIFE AND HORRID DEATH OF DR. JOHN FAUSTUS, THE.** n.d. (*c.* 1820, see note below). Lauriston, 2844(1) and 2850.A.(15), Cat. p. 75.

THE HISTORY OF / THE WICKED LIFE AND HORRID DEATH OF / DR. JOHN FAUSTUS, / SHEWING / HOW HE SOLD HIMSELF TO THE DEVIL TO HAVE POWER FOR / 24 YEARS TO DO WHAT HE PLEASED, / ALSO THE STRANGE THINGS DONE BY HIM AND / MEPHOSTOPHILES. / WITH AN ACCOUNT HOW THE DEVIL CAME FOR / HIM AT THE END OF 24 YEARS, AND / TORE HIM IN PIECES. / [woodcut] / PRINTED FOR J. LUMSDEN & SON, GLASGOW.

12 unsigned leaves. No woodcuts in text.

*A frequent subject for chapbooks. Lauriston lists some 14 editions and issues.*

The NLSc date this item as *c.* 1816. Either date could be correct. 157×94 mm. [BM; GlaUL; NLSc.]

**158. LAIRD OF COOL'S GHOST!, THE.** 1817. By 'The Rev. Mr. Ogilvie'. Lauriston 2844(3), p. 174.

Plate

THE / LAIRD OF COOL'S / GHOST! / BEING / A COPY OF SEVERAL CONFERENCES AND MEETINGS THAT / PAST BETWIXT THE REV. MR. OGILVIE, LATE MINISTER OF / THE GOSPEL AT INNERWICK IN EAST LOTHIAN, AND THE / GHOST OF MR. MAXWELL, LATE LAIRD OF COOL. / AS IT WAS FOUND IN MR. OGILVIE'S CLOSET AFTER HIS DEATH, / VERY SOON AFTER THESE CONFERENCES. / [WRITTEN BY HIS OWN HAND.] / [two woodcuts] / GLASGOW: / PUBLISHED BY J. LUMSDEN & SON. / [p.rule] / 1817.

12 unsigned leaves. Pp. 24. No woodcuts in text.

The left hand woodcut on the TP was used later in *The History of Duncan Campbell, 1822* (No. 154). See note in this item on the origin of the woodcut of the figure of the man.

*A very popular title. Lumsden published another edition in 1822 (see next item). Lauriston lists about 11 editions.*

*It is highly questionable whether the attribution of the story to Mr Ogilvie was not merely based on the statement on the TP that the 'copy of several conferences' was 'found in Mr. Ogilvie's Closet after his death, very soon after these Conferences' and 'written by his own hand' implying that the Powers of Darkness had a good deal to do with the*

THE

# LIFE

AND

## Surprising Adventures

OF

### *Sir William Wallace,*

THE

### Champion of Scotland.

GLASGOW:

Published by J. Lumsden & Son.

1822.

*160*: The Life ... of Sir William Wallace.

THE

LIFE AND TRANSACTIONS

OF

# Mrs. Jane Shore,

### Concubine to K. Edward 4th,

CONTAINING

An Account of her Parentage, Wit, and Beauty.
Her Marriage with Mr. SHORE. The King's
Vifits to her, her going to Court, and leaving
her Hufband. Her great Diftrefs and Mifery
after the King's Death, &c.

GLASGOW:

Publifhed by J. Lumfden and Son.

1816.

161: The Life and Transactions of Mrs. Jane Shore.

*writing and Mr Ogilvie's subsequent rapid demise; all of which would add a grisly attraction to the story.*
(Communicated.)
153×87 mm. [Aberdeen; NLSc.]

**159. LAIRD OF COOL'S GHOST!, THE.** 1822. By 'The Rev. Mr. Ogilvie'. Lauriston 2844(11).

THE / LAIRD OF / COOL'S GHOST. / BEING / A COPY OF SEVERAL CONFERENCES AND MEETINGS THAT / PASSED BETWIXT THE / REVEREND MR. OGILVIE, / LATE MINISTER OF THE GOSPEL AT INNERWICK, IN EAST / LOTHIAN, AND THE / GHOST OF MR. MAXWELL, / LATE LORD OF COOL. / AS IT WAS FOUND IN MR. OGILVIE'S CLOSET AFTER HIS / DEATH, VERY SOON AFTER THESE CONFERENCES. / WRITTEN WITH HIS OWN HAND. / [woodcut] / GLASGOW: / PUBLISHED BY J. LUMSDEN & SON. / [p.rule] / 1822.
12mo. 12 unsigned leaves. Pp. 24. No woodcuts in text. Imprint of J. Neilson at foot of p. 24. The title-page has similar text to the earlier edition but with a single woodcut on TP which was used for *Fun upon Fun* (No. 152) and the block is now much worn and cracked.
157×90 mm. [BM; GlaUL; NLSc.]

**160. LIFE AND SURPRISING ADVENTURES OF SIR WILLIAM WALLACE, THE.** 1822.
Plate
THE / LIFE / AND / SURPRISING ADVENTURES / OF / SIR WILLIAM WALLACE, / THE / CHAMPION OF SCOTLAND. / [woodcut] / GLASGOW: / PUBLISHED BY J. LUMSDEN & SON. / [p.rule] / 1822.
12 unsigned leaves. Pp. 24. Imprint of J. Neilson at foot of p. 24. No woodcuts in text.
*An immensely popular book. Lauriston list some 21 editions and issues.*
175×99 mm. [BM; CUL; UCLA.]

**161. LIFE AND TRANSACTIONS OF MRS. JANE SHORE, THE.** 1816. Lauriston 2844(2).
Plate
THE / LIFE AND TRANSACTIONS / OF / MRS. JANE SHORE, / CONCUBINE TO K. EDWARD 4th, / CONTAINING / AN ACCOUNT OF HER PARENTAGE, WIT, AND BEAUTY. / HER MARRIAGE WITH MR. SHORE. THE KING'S / VISITS TO HER, HER GOING TO COURT, AND

THE

# MASSACRE OF GLENCO.

### In a Letter from a Gentleman in Edinburgh to his Friend in London.

Giving a particular account of that unprecedented tranfaction, wherein orders were given that all the Males of the M'Donalds in that diftrict under 70 fhould be put to the Sword, in which 38 persons were killed in cold blood, moft of them in their bed, 900 Cows, 200 Horfes, and a great many Sheep and Goats were carried off to the Garrifon at Iverlochy, together with the extreme mifery, and death, of many of the women and children, in being deprived of their father and husbands, and driven from their homes in the most inclement and fevere seafon of the year.

"William R. As for MackIan of Glenco, and "that tribe, if they can be diftinguifhed from the rest "of the Highlanders, it will be proper, for the vindica- "tion of publie justice, to extirpate that set of thieves."

W. R.

14th Article of instructions, Jan. 16. 1692.

GLASGOW:
Publifhed by J. Lumsden and Son.
1819.

THE

*Merry and Diverting*

# EXPLOITS

OF

*George Buchanan,*

COMMONLY CALLED

The King's Fool.

· IN TWO PARTS.

GLASGOW,

PUBLISHED BY J. LUMSDEN & SON.

*164*: The Merry and Diverting Exploits of George Buchanan.

LEAVING / HER HUSBAND-HER GREAT DISTRESS AND MISERY / AFTER THE KING'S DEATH, &c. / [woodcut] / GLASGOW: / PUBLISHED BY J. LUMSDEN AND SON. / [p.rule] / 1816.

12 unsigned leaves. Pp. 24 [1,2] 3-24. No woodcuts in text. The TP woodcut is also used in No. 151.

*The earliest dated chapbook, except for* The Unfortunate Lovers, 1808 *(No. 169) which cost 6d. and is outside the normal run of Lumsden chapbooks. A very popular work. The BM. catalogue lists some dozen or so editions. Among other publishers of this title were Davison of Alnwick, 1825, and Richardson of Derby, 1845.*

149×89 mm. [NLSc.]

**162. MAGIC PILL, THE; OR, DAVIE AND BESS.** 1819. Lauriston 2850 A(14).

THE / MAGIC PILL; / OR, / DAVIE AND BESS. / A TALE. / [16 lines relating details of contents.] / [d.p.rule] / GLASGOW: / PUBLISHED BY J. LUMSDEN & SON. / [p.rule] / 1819.

4 unsigned leaves. Pp. [1,2] 3-8. No woodcuts.

(Communicated.)

169×99 mm. [NLSc.]

**163. MASSACRE OF GLENCO, THE.** 1819. Lauriston 2844 (4).

Plate

THE / MASSACRE OF GLENCO. / IN A LETTER FROM A GENTLEMAN IN EDINBURGH / TO HIS FRIEND IN LONDON. / [12 lines of text relating contents.] / "WILLIAM R. AS FOR MACKIAN OF GLENCO, AND / "THAT TRIBE, IF THEY CAN BE DISTINGUISHED FROM THE REST / "OF THE HIGHLANDERS, IT WILL BE PROPER, FOR THE VINDICA- / "TION OF PUBLIC JUSTICE, TO EXTIRPATE THAT SET OF THIEVES". / W.R. / 14TH ARTICLE OF INSTRUCTIONS, JAN. 16. 1692. / [p.s.rule] / GLASGOW: / PUBLISHED BY J. LUMSDEN AND SON. / 1819.

4 unsigned leaves. Pp. [1,2] 3-8. No woodcuts.

(Communicated.)

172×100 mm. [NLSc.]

**164. MERRY AND DIVERTING EXPLOITS OF GEORGE BUCHANAN, THE.** n.d. (*c.* 1820). Attributed to Dougal Graham. Fairley 230.

Plate

THE / MERRY AND DIVERTING / EXPLOITS / OF /

THE

## *MERRY TRICKS*

OF

# L E P E R

## THE TAYLOR.

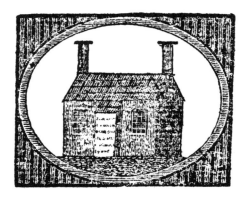

GLASGOW :

Published by J Lumsden & Son,

1822,

*165*: The Merry Tricks of Leper the Taylor.

THE

# ROYAL RIDDLE BOOK

A

## New Collection

OF

# RIDDLES,

FOR THE

*Entertainment of Youth.*

*Of merry Books this is the chief,*
*It is a purging Pill,*
*To carry off all heavy Grief,*
*And make you laugh your fill.*

GL SGOW.:
Published y J. LUMSDEN & SON.
1820.

*166*: The Royal Riddle Book.

GEORGE BUCHANAN, / COMMONLY CALLED / THE KING'S FOOL. / [p.rule] / IN TWO PARTS. / [p.rule] / [woodcut] / GLASGOW, / PUBLISHED BY J. LUMSDEN & SON.
12 unsigned leaves. Pp. 24. No woodcuts in text.
*Buchanan was a most popular subject for chapbooks; Lauriston lists some 35 editions of his exploits, sayings, jests, etc. For another Lumsden edition see No. 171.*
165×94 mm. [BM; Bodley.]

**165. MERRY TRICKS OF LEPER THE TAYLOR, THE.**
1822. Attributed to Dougal Graham.
Plate
THE / MERRY TRICKS / OF / LEPER / THE TAYLOR. / [woodcut] / GLASGOW: / PUBLISHED BY J. LUMSDEN & SON. / [p.rule] / 1822.
12mo. 12 unsigned leaves. Pp. 24. No woodcuts in text. Imprint of J. Neilson at foot of p. 24.
*A popular chapbook under various names and forms, such as* Fun upon Fun! or, the Comical . . . Tricks of Leper. . . . *(No. 152). And see Lauriston, sub* Graham, Dougal.
160×95 mm. [Bodley; GlaUL.]

**166. ROYAL RIDDLE BOOK, THE.** 1820.
Plate
THE / ROYAL RIDDLE BOOK. / A / NEW COLLECTION / OF / RIDDLES, / FOR THE / ENTERTAINMENT OF YOUTH. / [four lines of verse] / [woodcut] / GLASGOW: / Published by J. Lumsden & Son. / 1820.
12 unsigned leaves. Pp. 24. Neilson's imprint at the foot of p. 24. No woodcuts in text. The TP woodcut used also in *Thrummy Cap and the Ghaist* (No. 168). The block is worn and deeply cracked, evidence of much use and careless handling.
165×95 mm. [Aberdeen; BM; Harvard.]

**167. THRUMMY CAP; A TALE.** n.d. (*c.* 1820). Lauriston, p. 31.
THRUMMY CAP; / A TALE. / [d.p.rule] / TO WHICH ARE ADDED, / YOUNG WHIP STITCH, / AND, / THE GIG DEMOLISHED. / [wavy rule] / GLASGOW: / PRINTED BY J. LUMSDEN & SON.
12 unsigned leaves. Pp. 24. No woodcuts.
*For notes on the authorship of the three stories see next item. This appears to be an earlier edition than No. 168, the latter having an*

# THRUMMY CAP

### AND THE

# GHAIST,

## A Diverting Tale.

#### To which are added,

## *YOUNG WHIP-STITCH,*

#### AND

## The Gig Demolished.

GLASGOW:
Published by J Lumsden & Son.
1824.

*167*: Thrummy Cap and the Ghaist.

*improved and more attractive TP, but there is no weight of evidence either way.*
162×95 mm. [Aberdeen; BM; Bodley; NLSc.]

## 168. THRUMMY CAP AND THE GHAIST. ? 1822 (see note below).
Plate
THRUMMY CAP / AND THE / GHAIST, / A DIVERTING TALE. / TO WHICH ARE ADDED, / YOUNG WHIP-STITCH, / AND / THE GIG DEMOLISHED. / [woodcut] / GLASGOW: / PUBLISHED BY J. LUMSDEN & SON. / [p.rule] / 182–.
12 unsigned leaves. Pp. 24. No woodcuts in text. Imprint of J. Neilson at foot of p. 24. The TP woodcut used also in *The Royal Riddle Book* (No. 166). The last figure in the date on the TP is broken, and the preceding figure deformed. '1822' is probably what was intended.
*A popular title; Lauriston lists some 14 editions. The authorship of* Thrummy Cap *has been disputed. BM General Catalogue gives it to Mrs Barbauld, but William Harvey in* Scottish Chapbook Literature *(Paisley, 1903), gives it to John Burness, a relative of Burns (p. 66, footnote), and is followed by Lauriston. The heading at p. 19 reads* THE GIG DEMOLISHED; / A POEM, / BY MRS BARBAULD. *I have found no other authority for this attribution; the poem is ignored by writers on Mrs Barbauld.* Young Whip-Stitch *is assigned to Mrs Barbauld by Bodley.*
    *The TP woodcut is in even worse condition than in* The Riddle Book; *it seems to have been broken in two, or at all events cracked from top to bottom, and in some impressions there appear signs of attempts to re-work the block, to no good effect.*
156×87 mm. [GlaUL.]

## 169. UNFORTUNATE LOVERS, THE. 1808. Price 6*d.*
THE UNFORTUNATE LOVERS, / OR / AFFECTING HIS-TORY / OF / MISS POLLY HAWKINS, / WHO RESIDED NEAR / BRENTFORD, MIDDLESEX, / AND / WILLIAM JONES, / FROM / LEEDS IN YORKSHIRE. / [d.p.rule] / [4 line quote] / [d.p.rule] / LONDON: / PRINTED AND SOLD BY J. BAILEY, 116, CHANCERY LANE, / AND MAY BE HAD OF MOST BOOKSELLERS. / ALSO BY MESSRS. LUMSDENS, GLASGOW. / PRICE 6d. / [p.rule] / 1808.
In 6's [a A-B⁶ C⁴]. 17 leaves. Pp. 32. FP of whole page woodcut of Polly Hawkins, hand-coloured, with 4 lines of text.
*A 'Gothic Chapbook', one of the numerous Gothic type novelettes*

THE

*Witty and Entertaining*

# EXPLOITS

OF

## GEORGE BUCHANAN,

COMMONLY CALLED

### THE KING'S FOOL.

IN TWO PARTS.

GLASGOW:

Publifhed by J. Lumsden & Son.

1822.

*171*: The Witty and Entertaining Exploits of George Buchanan.

*published by J. Bailey and several others at 6d. with a coloured frontispiece (sometimes folding). They were almost invariably of 24 pp. Though generally common enough, no others with the Lumsden imprint have been found and this may be an isolated case. Lumsden was probably acting as Scottish agent to boost northern sales.*
175×103 mm. [Renier (disbound; usually issued in plain light or dark blue wrappers).]

## 170. VISIONS, DISCOVERIES, AND WARNINGS, &C, THE. 1820. Lauriston 2844(7), Cat. p. 185.

THE / VISIONS, DISCOVERIES, AND WARNINGS / OF THE / DREADFUL AND TERRIBLE JUDGEMENTS / UPON / SCOTLAND, ENGLAND, AND IRELAND, / WHICH WERE REVEALED TO / JOHN PORTER OF CROSSIBEIG. / TAKEN FROM HIS OWN MOUTH, ( WHILE CONFINED / TO HIS BED, BEING BLIND) AND ATTESTED BY HIM- / SELF, AS BY HIS DECLARATION ANNEXED. / JOEL. ii. 28, 30, 31, 32. / [8 line quotation] / [swelled rule] / GLASGOW: / PUBLISHED BY J. LUMSDEN & SON. / [p.rule] / 1820.
12 unsigned leaves. Pp. 24. No woodcuts.
(Communicated.)
170×95 mm. [Aberdeen; NLSc.]

## 171. WITTY AND ENTERTAINING EXPLOITS OF GEORGE BUCHANAN, THE. 1822. Lauriston 2844 (13), Cat. p. 28.

Plate
THE / WITTY AND ENTERTAINING / EXPLOITS / OF / GEORGE BUCHANAN, / COMMONLY CALLED / THE KING'S FOOL. / IN TWO PARTS. / [woodcut] / GLASGOW: / PUBLISHED BY J. LUMSDEN & SON. / [p.rule] / 1822.
12mo. 12 unsigned leaves. Pp. 24 . No woodcuts in text. A very popular subject for chapbooks. See note to another Lumsden edition *The Merry and Diverting Exploits of George Buchanan.* No. 164.
*The TP woodcut, the block now much damaged and cracked right through, was also used in* Comical Transactions of Lothian Tom. *No. 149.*
156×88 mm. [GlaUL; NLSc.]

**YOUNG WHIP-STITCH.** See Nos. 167 and 168.

# APPENDIX: NON-JUVENILE

**172. PILGRIM'S PROGRESS, THE.** By John Bunyan. n.d. (1857).

Ornamental title-page: THE / PILGRIMS / PROGRESS / BY / JOHN BUNYAN. / ILLUMINATED / GLASGOW / JAMES LUMSDEN & SON. / [All within an illuminated panel at lower right of title-page.] Both the title and the elaborate pictorial ornamentation of the page, including a scroll lettered 'Knock and it shall be opened to you', are lithographed in colours and signed by H[ugh] Wilson, Glasgow.

Quarto. In fours. 204 leaves.

First leaf blank [unnumbered], front and lithographed title-page [unnumbered], p. [i] [Section title]. The Pilgrim's Progress, Part I. Illuminated [printed in green within a decorative strapwork frame — possibly a soft metal engraving]. p. [ii] Blank, pp. [iii]-xxiv. [Preface.] The Life of John Bunyan by the Rev. Thomas Scott. p. [1] Text commences under an elaborate woodcut headpiece 'The Pilgrim's Progress. Part I.' [Engraved by G. Dalziel after T. Watt], pp. 2-189, p. [190] conclusion. p. [191] [Section title] The Pilgrim's Progress, Part II. Illuminated. [as for Part I but printed in pink], p. [192] blank, pp. [193]-200 The Author's Way of sending forth his second part . . ., p. [201] [Text part II commences under a woodcut headpiece 'The Pilgrim's Progress. Part II.' Engraved by E. Dalziel], pp. 202-374, p. [375] List of Illustrations, p. [376] Decorated final page. Final leaf blank.

Illustrations: Frontispiece: John Bunyan. W. S. Wilkinson after W. Sharp. Printed Glasgow: Mackenzie White, & Co. [Inserts] Facing p. 37 [Pilgrim at the Cross. Engraved by George Dalziel]; p. 77 [Pilgrim Christ and Moses. Engraved by E. Dalziel]; p. 185 [City. Engraved by E. Dalziel]; p. 207 [Christian dreaming. Engraved by George Dalziel]; p. 287 [Lions. Engraved by George Dalziel]; p. 363 [Christian arrives. Engraved by E. Dalziel]. All after William Harvey. p. [iii] decorated initial. E. Evans after G. F. Sargent; p. xvi. Bunyan's House. E. Evans after G. F. Sargent. [Woodcuts in text] p. 4 [Pilgrim fleeing. E. Evans after G. F. Sargent]; p. 21. [Pilgrim approaches gate. E. Dalziel after T. Watt [?]; p. 42. [P. in arbour. E.D. after T.W.]; p. 46 [Lions. E.D.]; p. 96 [Evangelist. E.D.]; p. 103 [Vanity Fair. E.D.]; p. 129 [Giant Despair. G.D.]; p. 153 [Net. E.D.]; p. 183 [Pool. E.D.]; p. 189. Unsigned decoration; p. 221. [Christian at the gate. E. Evans after G. F. Sargent]; p. 265. [Joseph catechized.

G.D.]; p. 280. [Mr Great-Heart. G.D.]; p. 318 [Giant slain. G.D.]; p. 341 [Mr Great-Heart. E.D.]; p. 374. [Finis motif in blue, signed ANDREW B.L.]; p. [376] [Decorative 'W' motif in blue, centred within a standard 'holly' border in blue].

[Woodcut borders] Almost every page of the book is framed by an elaborately decorated woodcut border, occasionally with metal rules added. These borders have a variety of characteristics but tend to be grouped in runs that correspond to one or more signatures of the book. They are printed in a variety of colours and the principal motifs are Diamond, Square, Holly, Angels, Snowflake and Serpentine.

Binding: Very dark maroon morocco, with elaborate gilt pictorial titling on spine. Front heavily decorated in gilt and colour; back less heavily decorated in gilt. Pale blue endpapers with floral design in gilt. Binder's label: Rowley & Evans ... Hatton Garden.

280×203 mm. [Brian Alderson (to whom we are indebted for the above details); Moon.]

# LUMSDEN'S 'SERIES' OF BOOKS

What induced Lumsdens to start these 'series' of books, beyond a vague idea of increasing sales, it is hard to see. For the greater part it came to nothing. Sometimes the books were named (often on the wrappers) as part of a 'series': the 'Children's Library', the 'Juvenile Library', 'The improved Edition of coloured Two-penny Books', or were grouped together under prices: Lumsden's Halfpenny Books, Twopenny Books and so on. Details of these are set out below. Only numbers 1 and 3 can be said to form a coherent 'series' and why numbers 2, 4 and 5 were grouped as 'series' it is impossible to say. The whole thing seems to point to feeble attempts to raise circulation by vague suggestions of more to follow, then abandoned for lack of material or just forgotten or thrown aside as not worth following up. Lack of any sort of general planning or editorial supervision is indicated, but this is not surprising as Lumsden's main business was stationery and the issue of books was very much a subsidiary activity.

1. LUMSDEN'S SUPERIOR EDITION OF PENNY BOOKS. Numbers 10, 63, etc. These are uniform in size (*c.* 129×76 mm.), format and (probably) date. They are all well-known stories except *The Juvenile Learner*. None is dated, but a likely period is 1830-40. Each book comprises 6 unsigned leaves, inclusive of the paper wrappers. The title-page is on the recto of the front wrapper in each case, with a woodcut; on the verso of the back wrapper is a variant repetition of the title-page, with a woodcut. Six of these books are in the British Library volume lettered 'Chap-Books' (which they are not), CH 810/169.

2. LUMSDEN'S JUVENILE LIBRARY. Numbers 59, 62 and 84. These seem to have nothing in common.

3. LUMSDEN & SON'S IMPROVED EDITION OF COL-OURED TWOPENNY BOOKS. Numbers 46, 47, etc. Mostly well-known stories, *Sinbad, The Forty Thieves*, etc. All late productions anywhere between 1830 and 1850, none dated.

4. LUMSDEN & SON'S CHILDREN'S LIBRARY. Numbers 29, 36, 43, etc. Two titles are divinity, the rest familiar titles such as *Gulliver*, etc. All cost 6*d.* Some are dated 1807 or before, but one is 1819.

5. LUMSDEN'S TOY BOOK MANUFACTORY. Numbers 9, 24, 29, etc. A mixed lot, with no apparent common nexus; ranges from *Abridgment of the Holy Bible, c.* 1805, and *The History of Joseph and his Brethren, c.* 1815-20 to *John Gilpin,* 1808 or before, and *Sandford & Merton c.* 1805. Priced from 1*d.* to 6*d.*

6. LUMSDEN & SON'S SUPERIOR EDITION OF HALFPENNY BOOKS, containing 16 pages each. Numbers 8, 11, 48, 139, etc. A mixed bag containing some instructional books as well as popular titles such as *History of Whittington and his Cat.* A 'series' of 12 titles are advertised on the back wrapper of each booklet. Although now extremely scarce they must have been a popular series — they were generously illustrated — *The House that Jack Built* with a woodcut on each page. Probably about 1820.

7. BOOKS PUBLISHED BY ROSS OF EDINBURGH, BUT TAKEN OVER BY LUMSDEN AND BEARING THEIR NAME. Numbers 20, 37, 38, etc. Lumsden's name usually appears on the upper cover, with the legend 'From Ross's Juvenile Library'. For further discussion of this, see the Introduction.

# BIBLIOGRAPHICAL WORKS REFERRED TO

CBEL. *The New Cambridge Bibliography of English Literature.* 1969-77.

Clouston, W. A. *Hieroglyphic Bibles.* 1894.

Darton, F. J. Harvey. *Children's Books in England.* 2nd ed. 1958.

Fairley, John A. *Dougal Graham & the Chapbooks by and attributed to him, with a bibliography.* 1914.

Gumuchian. *Livres de l'Enfance du XVe au XIXe Siècle ... en vente à la Libraire Gumuchian et Cie. 2 vols.* 1930.

Lauriston. *Catalogue of the Lauriston Castle Chapbooks in the National Library of Scotland.* 1964.

Hugo, Rev. Thomas. *The Bewick Collector.* 2 vols. 1866. 1868.

Lisney, A. A. *Bibliography of British Lepidoptera.* 1960.

Moon, Mrs E. M. *John Harris's Books for Youth, 1801-1843. A Check-list.* 1976.

NBL. *Children's Books of Yesterday.* A Catalogue, prepared by Mr Percy Muir, of an exhibition at the National Book League, 1946.

Opie, I & P. *Oxford Dictionary of Nursery Rhymes.* 1951.

Osborne. *The Osborne Collection of Early Children's Books.* Prepared by Judith St. John. 2 vols. Vol. I. 1958; Vol. II. 1975.

Roscoe, Sydney. *Bibles, Early English, Scottish & Irish Thumb.* Article in *The Book Collector.* Summer, 1973.

Roscoe, Sydney. *John Newbery & his Successors. 1740-1814.* 1973.

Spielmann & Layard. *Kate Greenaway.* 1905.

Welch, Dr d'Alté A. *Bibliography of American Children's Books printed prior to 1820.* The American Antiquarian Society, Proceedings, 1963-7.

# AUTHORS

This list comprises all authors, whether known or writing pseudonymously, suggested, fictitious or obviously invented *ad hoc* (e.g. Tiffany Tarbottle).

# INDEX OF TITLES

*Books are listed under the principal word in the full title.*